Robert A. Fit C000099199

# Outcast
# But Not Forsaken

Robert A. Fitzharris

# PARAGUAY
## SOUTH AMERICA

One inch equals 135 miles
approximately

BOLIVIA

BRAZIL

Gran Chaco

Colonia Mennonita
• FILADELFIA

Puerto
Casado •

Rio Paraguay

• CONCEPCIÓN

Nueva
Germania

Rosario •

Friesland
☐ **PRIMAVERA**

ASUNCION ●

San Bernadino

**SAPUCAY**
☐   • VILLARICA

Nueva
Italia

Colonia
Independencia

Iguazu
Falls

ARGENTINA

Rio Paraná

─ 𝒩 ─

ENCARNACIÓN
●

CORRIENTES
●

Rio Paraná

ARGENTINA

To
BUENOS AIRES
and
MONTEVIDEO

# Outcast
# But Not Forsaken

## True Stories From a Paraguayan Leper Colony

### Collected by Maureen Burn

PLOUGH PUBLISHING HOUSE
HUTTERIAN BRETHREN
Rifton, New York, USA
Robertsbridge, England

© 1986 by the Plough Publishing House of
The Woodcrest Service Committee, Inc.
Hutterian Brethren
Rifton, NY 12471, USA

Robertsbridge, E. Sussex TN32 5DR, England

The Illustrators of this book include:

DOÑA MARIA
*with drawings mostly done after Maria was over 80 years old*
VICTOR CRAWLEY
ELNA BLOUGH
LESLIE HOLLAND
STANLEY FLETCHER
DON PETERS

Library of Congress Cataloging-in-Publication Data

Outcast, but not forsaken.

Based on conversations with Doña María.
1. María, Doña. 2. Lepers—Germany—Biography.
3. Lepers—Paraguay—Biography. 4. Missions to
lepers—Paraguay. I. Burn, Maureen, 1905–
RC154.55.P3M376   1986   362.1'969'9800924 [B]      86-25169
ISBN 0-87486-184-5

ISBN 0-87486-184-5
Printed at the Deer Spring Press
Hutterian Brethren
Norfolk, CT, USA

*Contents*

# Part 1

## A VISIT TO SAPUCAY
(By Way of Introduction)

# Part 2
## IF I MAKE MY BED IN HELL, THOU ART THERE
Ps. 139:8

# Contents

## Part 3

### GOD IS OVER ALL

(As recorded by Maureen Burn* and Belinda Manley**)

*Many drawings in this book (marked Doña Maria or M) are the work of Maria herself
mostly drawn after she was over 80 years old*

## FOREWORD

This book has an unusual history. It is the result, in 1986, of combining and editing several manuscripts written by Maureen Burn in Paraguay during 1954-1958. Part 1 is based largely on Maureen's account of her visit to Sapucay. She called it "The Furnace." A shorter version of this was published by the Wheathill Bruderhof in England in 1957 (*Plough* magazine, Volume 5, No. 1) under the title "Visit to a Leper Colony." Parts 2 and 3 are a combination of Maureen's unpublished manuscripts "If I Make My Bed in Hell . . . " and "Parables from the Underworld," with a few additional anecdotes recorded by Belinda Manley. All this material is based on conversations with "Doña Maria," as she talked naturally in her simple Spanish to sisters of the Sociedad de Hermanos (Society of Brothers), when they visited her in her little hut near Primavera Hospital. We are thankful to Maureen and Belinda for recording and preserving Maria's vivid memories of Sapucay.

Our thanks go also to Major Jenty Fairbank, Archivist at the International Headquarters of the Salvation Army in London, for more information about Ambrosio Castillo published in *All the World* magazine in 1965, which we have incorporated in the Epilogue.

We are deeply touched by the simple faith of some of these men and women who were treated as outcasts by society. They come alive in these unpretentious narratives and have much to teach us. We publish these accounts now with the agreement of Maureen and Belinda, giving God the glory.

Hutterian Brethren                                                    THE EDITORS

*Campo Dolores, Primavera, Paraguay.*      V.C.

# Part 1

## A VISIT TO SAPUCAY
### (By Way of Introduction)

V.C.

# A VISIT TO SAPUCAY

## (By Way of Introduction)

In July 1954 we welcomed at our bruderhof community in Paraguay, South America, the first person from a leprosy settlement to come and live with us. The joy was increased because this led to the reuniting of a family separated for nearly twenty years, the husband and son having come to the Bruderhof about ten years earlier. At first, Maria lived in an isolation house near our hospital, but when it was established that the illness had been checked, she was able to live among us normally. Her coming meant not only a widening of our sympathies but first-hand acquaintance with one who had shared the lot of a people "living without the camp."

Our community of Hutterian Brethren in Paraguay, known as Colonia Primavera, was established in 1941 and existed until 1961, when most of the members moved to communities in the United States, England, or Germany. Although a small plane could fly from Asuncion, the capital of Paraguay, to Primavera in about half an hour, the journey by land involved an overnight riverboat trip of about fourteen hours up the broad Rio Paraguay and, in good weather, another fourteen hours by horse wagon into the interior (in later years four or five hours by truck from the river). Primavera Hospital was built in 1942 and staffed by members of the Hutterian Brethren. Maria came there for an operation. On July 8, 1954 she was brought in a small plane, accompanied by one of our brothers, from the Santa Isabel Colony near Sapucay, about forty miles southeast of Asuncion. My own work at that time was in the hospital laboratory, and that is where I first met Maria and began to note down the true stories that follow, told to me in her very simple Spanish.

At Maria's invitation I accompanied her when after some eighteen months in Primavera she returned to the leper colony to settle her affairs before coming to the Bruderhof for good. One morning toward the end of 1955 Maria and I set off. We drove in our truck to Puerto Rosario on the Rio Paraguay and from there took the overnight riverboat to Asuncion.

3

Here we were met by Peter Mathis, a member of our community, who was to accompany us to the Santa Isabel Colony near Sapucay on the following day. Another member had already visited the doctor who was director of the colony. (He lived in Asuncion and flew out to the colony to treat the patients.) He had promised to arrange for a horse to be brought out from the colony to meet Maria at Sapucay station, so that she could ride the six miles to the colony.

So Peter and I borrowed *maletas* ("saddlebags") and packed our things into them, as they are the best means of carrying belongings on horseback. We also took food for a three-days' stay: *galletas* ("hardtack") and cheese and corned beef and yerba maté—the latter especially for Maria. It is her remedy for tiredness, headache, or indigestion; also it warms her in cold weather and cools her in hot weather. We also each took a poncho or blanket.

Then next morning we took the train to Sapucay. It was my first experience of a train journey in Paraguay, and I shall never forget it. The fuel for the engine was wood. The train had a long corridor down the center, and this was filled with a constant stream of vendors milling their way back and forth from end to end of the train. There were old women with pastries or chunks of *asado* ("roast meat") or crocheted bedcovers, young girls with baskets of *chipa* (bread with cheese and egg incorporated in it), small urchins selling water or *tereré* (maté made with cold water and sucked through a bombilla or metal sucking tube), and one jolly fuzzy-haired, dark-skinned little bootblack—probably a Brazilian. The *tereré* boys carried a can of water with an improvised handle. They also carried a small cloth bag of dry yerba maté hung on a cord from their necks, and an enamel cup and bombilla. I noticed some passengers bought only water and others ordered a cup of *tereré*. The boy made this by pouring cold water on dry yerba in the cup. Then the boy stuck his bombilla in it and gave it to the customer. When the customer had finished, the boy tipped the old yerba leaves out of the window and rinsed the cup out with some of his water, and it was ready for the next customer. Often when handling change the boy stuck the bombilla in his own mouth to free a hand for counting. I noticed that when the *tereré* boys had sold out, they were able to buy a nice dinner for themselves from the selling women—*asado* or *chipa*. They also probably had a little money over to take home.

The scenery was most interesting, as it was different from the flat and more tropical part of Paraguay that I knew. We passed San Bernardino on the left. It is a kind of inland holiday place—a lake—for the Asuncion people.

*San Bernardino, Paraguay.*                                              *V.C.*

Peter asked a small boy how soon we would be in Sapucay. The boy whispered to the others, and all left the compartment where we were. They probably thought we were new patients going to the colony there.

When we arrived at Sapucay station, we began to look out for the horse promised for Maria. We saw several men with horses, but Maria did not recognize any of them, and anyway they were passing on and not waiting for anyone.

Peter then went off to try and hire horses for us or a wagon, but he was told no one wanted to hire anything on a Saturday afternoon. Maria said she was quite prepared to walk in slow stages, but we did not want to do this. Peter then found the name of a German who is friendly to our community; so he went to ask his advice. In half an hour he came back with an oxen wagon. The German had found a man who had not yet unyoked his oxen and was willing to take us. The oxen were tired, as they had been carting alfalfa most of the day. I felt sorry for them, but the man let them go at their own pace, which was half as fast as a man walking, so that it took us four hours to do six miles.

We followed a dirt track out of the village of Sapucay. When we got beyond the village, we passed a few straggling houses and saw people peep round the doorway or round the corner, as if almost afraid of contagion, for were we not strangers going toward the leper colony? One man called to the wagoner in Guaraní, and he answered. Maria said the man was asking about us, and the wagoner had replied, "I can't get information out of them; they are talking a gringo (foreign) tongue." We had been talking in German.

The cottages had now stopped, and we entered a wide, grass-grown road with fences along both sides and woods coming right up to the fence. The road twisted and turned and climbed all the time between wooded hills. It was a wonderful moonlit night. The slow pace of the oxen allowed all the impressions time to sink in: the silvery light, the moving oxen, the grassy road with the shadow of the trees on it, and the moon suddenly appearing over the purple shoulder of a hill. I could not help thinking that we were passing along a via dolorosa, and that the uncanny beauty of the scene contrasted sadly with the heavy hearts that had passed along that way.

Suddenly the wagon pulled up. We had arrived. There was nothing to indicate it—no high walls or barbed wire enclosure. All we saw was a light fence such as might form the boundary of a large ranch. There was a farm gate leading into the colony, and it was open. Outside the fence there were two houses, one of adobe and the other of brick. The adobe one was the administration house, and the brick one was the doctor's house, where he lived when visiting the colony.

A young man came out of the administration house and greeted "Doña Maria" very warmly. Maria said he is a male nurse in the hospital, but he also disinfects letters and helps in the administration. He said he would try and find accommodation for us. Seemingly, relatives of patients usually sleep in the patients' houses when on a visit. There is no accommodation for visitors, though probably important visitors coming with the doctor would be put up in the doctor's house.

We said we wanted to accompany Maria to her house, so the male nurse said he would send two soldiers with us to show us the way back. The soldiers did not utter one word to us. They walked on in front and did not offer to carry anything. Peter and I helped Maria to carry her things. She had brought a nice lot of presents of clothing for her friends, as well as her own blankets and clothes. We passed through an open gate and into a wood. The trees met overhead, and we could not see. It felt as though we were walking along a dried-up stream, as we were always stumbling over boulders and stones. It took us about ten minutes to pass through this belt of woodland, which separates the "healthy" part of the colony from the "sick" part.

As soon as we were out of it, we saw the first houses, each with a little plot of land. Some were nicely cultivated with maize, and others were a wilderness of *yuyos* ("weeds"). The houses varied in size and condition according to the means of the owner. They had been built by the patients themselves and were mostly of the Paraguayan type, that is, one room with walls and one without walls, thatched over with the same roof, and with mud floors. Some had a nice veranda, which was used as a living room. Maria told me that everyone preferred the freedom of a little house, however small, to the institutionalism of either the hospital or the *salas* ("dormitories"). All new patients have to go to the *salas* to begin with, till they manage to get or build a little house, or share one with someone else.

Doña M.

Only those who cannot attend to themselves or lack means to procure a hut make their home in the hospital.

It was now about 8:30 p.m., and most people were indoors or in bed. Maria told us that most people went to bed with the sun in order to save candles or kerosene.

Maria got quite excited as we went along. She pointed to a small house set back on the left and said, "Florenciana lives there. She has been keeping my calf for me." Then we passed a house on the right, and there was a light shining indoors. Maria said, "Felipa lives there. I used to live with her," and she called out, "Felipa." Felipa came out and immediately said, *"Ah, Doña Maria, qué gorda!"* ("Ah, Doña Maria, how stout you are!")

This is a compliment, and everyone said it to Maria. Maria, who had actually put on weight since coming to us, said on the other hand how thin everyone looked. This was because the *cooperativa* had stopped running, and people had lost the vegetables it grew and the money they used to earn on the land. (For a number of years the joint United States-Paraguayan service, *Servicio Técnico Interamericano de Cooperación Agrícola*, or STICA, ran a primitive farm program at Santa Isabel to grow some crops and also provide work for the patients. This was known in the colony as the *cooperativa*.) Also bread was scarce because of the political troubles between Paraguay and Argentina, so that wheat had nearly ceased coming into Paraguay.

Felipa was so keen to hear all Maria's news that we could hardly get away. However, we were all tired, so we decided not to call on anyone else on the way to Maria's house.

We passed the Roman Catholic church, a stone building built by the patients with material supplied to them. Then we passed the nuns' house and the two *pabellones* (men's wing and women's wing of the hospital), kitchen, and pharmacy. All this complex was fenced in to protect it from the patients' cattle, which graze in common on the prairie land and wander at will round their owners' houses.

We then crossed a soccer field and came to the storehouse, where the people queue up for stores, and the *calabozo* ("jail") adjoining it. Jail is looked on as a bit of a joke. The prisoner can go out for walks with his wife or friends during the day, but he must be locked in at night. He can have visitors and watch the soccer matches and share a bombilla with his warders, who are also patients. People are put in the *calabozo* for being found drunk (*caña*—the native rum—is forbidden in theory), or for stealing from the storehouse, or for offences against young girls, or for leaving the colony without permission.

Some yards beyond this, Maria stopped. She pointed to a stile leading to two houses, and she said, "The first house is mine and the next is Mauricio's. He has the key of my house, but he has his evening meal at the Valenzuelas' house with some other young men. Marina and José Valenzuela are an elderly couple, and Marina cooks for the single men. That's her house there." Maria went and called Mauricio and said she wanted her key. The whole group came out and gave Maria a great welcome, and she went in to the Valenzuelas' to have some supper. I offered to give her the yerba I was carrying for her in my saddlebag, but Maria said, "Oh, they will give me some if they have it." "Have you some yerba?" she called out. "Yes," they said, "there is no need to unpack the saddlebag." We said "Good night" to Maria and returned. The soldiers walked in silence behind us.

The young man who had received us at the administration house showed us where we could sleep. He told Peter he could have a bed in the *galpón* ("shed") where the soldiers slept, and I was given a bed in a little hay barn at the back of the young man's house.

Next morning the commissary came along and gave us each a permit to enter the colony. He said we must give them to the nuns on entry and call for them again on leaving. With these in hand we set off and covered the same route we had stumbled along the night before in the dark. We got through the belt of wood and were just admiring a particularly tidy house with a vegetable garden and rosebushes, when the couple smiled at us. They were sitting at a table on the veranda with a dog lying contentedly at their feet. We shouted, "*Buenos días* ['good day']!" and they immediately came to the gate to talk to us. We said we had come with Doña Maria. They were most interested, and the woman said to the man, "Didn't I tell you it was Doña Maria's voice last night passing our door?" We could hardly get away from them, and it was the same with all others whom we greeted. Many of them asked, "Could we not also come to your settlement?"

Then we came to the Roman Catholic church. It was Sunday morning, and we heard the sound of singing coming from it. It seemed to be a Guaraní melody, unfamiliar to European ears but very haunting. It seemed to express a sense of longing, a yearning upward. We slowed our pace and listened as we passed in silence.

The nuns' house is a stone building lying between the church and the hospital. We knocked, and a French nun came out. She stamped our permits and kept them. We asked her where she came from, and she said "Havre." We said, "You are far from home." "That is all the better for our kind of work," said she. She was a young woman, obviously well educated, with golden brown eyes and a dignified reserve of manner. I felt she was happy and had found fulfillment in her work. The four nuns who do such selfless service there belong to the Little Sisters of St. Vincent de Paul, who dedicate their lives to the care of leprosy patients.

We left the nun and proceeded toward Maria's house. We noticed that the nicely built hospital *pabellones* and all the other American-built buildings had plaques attached saying, "This is a gift from the American nation." As we passed the *pabellones*, we noticed a strong smell of sulphur (though the prevailing odor of the colony was that of wood fires), and I remembered that Maria had once told me that some patients say no snake will bite a patient having sulfa drug treatment, because it dislikes sulphur.

We passed a small stone building further on, which also had an American plaque on it. The Americans had built it as a bath house, but water was too short, so it was used now and then for shutting up an occasional case in solitary confinement.

Some yards past the stone bath house we came to the stile leading to Maria's house. As we approached her house, we were met by the sweet scent of a large overgrown rosebush. This was the famous *rosa blanca* ("white rose"), of which Maria had often spoken. Its petals, if put in your yerba maté are a very good purifier of the blood. She had given cuttings to nearly everyone in the colony, and she was going to bring a bundle of cuttings back with her to Primavera.

I was just telling Peter about the rosebush when Maria herself came out and brought her neighbor Mauricio to meet us. He had looked after the house in her absence. We both took a strong liking to this young man. Maria had said of him that he could not be hypocritical and would have nothing to do with any religious observance in which he did not believe. We felt the same about him. Mauricio was thirty years old and had been told he had leprosy when he was doing his military service, aged nineteen. He had been at the colony ever since. He had at one time wanted to marry a girl, Dorotea, at the colony, but the girl was under the influence of the nuns, who told her she should not marry a freethinker.

Mauricio lives with another young man, Candido, who was a student and is an Evangelical. Both have suffered for their convictions in not being able to marry. Candido told us no girl in the colony would marry him because of his faith.

The old couple Valenzuela were there and several other people we did not know. One man came just to buy Maria's calf. He said, "I am going to register it under the name of 'Primavera.'" Maria had thought that if she sold her cow and her calf and one or two other things, that would pay for her journey. Peter and I did not like taking the money for more than that, as the folk were so poor. Maria had thought out beforehand what cooking pots or other items she would give to the very poorest, and this she did. None of the richer people wanted a house like hers of the campesino style, and the poor who would have wanted it had no money. Maria told Peter he could do as he liked with her house, as she wanted to settle her affairs and join us. So Peter gave everything into Mauricio's hands. (Later the Brotherhood told Peter to write Mauricio and say he should use it all as he saw fit to help the folk who needed it, and that is how it was settled.) Peter went off with Mauricio and the student to their house nearby, and I stayed with Maria.

Dorotea came to visit Maria, and Maria gave her a nice dress, which was an exact fit. Dorotea was delighted. Then Dorotea wanted to buy a big wooden chest of Maria's for a small sum. She wanted to take it with her, so I said I would come and help her. It had a handle at each end and was a bargain, she said, but she had no money on her. This was the girl I mentioned earlier. She was now married to a Roman Catholic. I said to Dorotea, "Why not bring the money to Doña Maria later?" She said she would (which she did) and was very pleased. As I went, she said, "I will pray for you."

Maria had so many visitors that Peter and I decided to leave her to them. It also was threatening to rain, and Paraguayan rain is usually a deluge, so we took our leave and went back to the *galpón* or soldiers' dormitory.

On the way a woman came out of her house to greet us. She told us she was Maria's friend Vicenta, so I at once knew who she was. She is a very firm Protestant and suffers in consequence. She asked me if I read the Bible. I said, "Yes, and I often go and read it with Maria." "Do you read the Bible?" she said to Peter. "Yes," said he. "Shake hands, brother!

Doña M.

Shake hands, sister!" she said. I felt ashamed to think how easy it is for us to read the Bible, whereas with them it is done at a cost. We also noticed that her hand had a permanent tremor.

We hastened on, because the rain was beginning to fall and Peter was wearing his poncho, which was his blanket for the night as well. We ate some rice with pieces of meat in it and *galletas* with the soldiers, and then Peter found a Spanish magazine with an article on the Santa Isabel Colony in it. We read it with interest. It dwelt on sensational items such as, "There are six murderers among the patients. . . . It is considered that confinement in a leprosarium is equivalent to penal servitude for life, so there are no further restrictions on them." Peter said the soldiers had been trying to read a Spanish newspaper and could barely read. Illiteracy is very prevalent in Paraguay. It poured with rain all the rest of the afternoon and evening, so we decided to get to bed early.

Next day (Monday) we visited Maria again, and she took us to see Apolinario Caceres. There is nothing planned about the layout of the little dwellings. They spring up anywhere—where there is a suitable flat spot, or where there are some shade trees, or by a termite heap, which will make a nice oven. Maria says some termite heaps can't be moved, so the house is built next to them. After zigzagging along several little footpaths and through one or two stiles (to keep out the wandering cows), we came to a small one-roomed house with a veranda in front and two or three benches in front of the veranda. There was a trellis with a vine growing on it, which formed a bit of shade for the benches, also a tree shaped like an umbrella. This was the place where the small group of Protestants meet every Sunday morning and where one or two inquirers come to Apolinario to be taught to read in order to be able to read the Bible.

Apolinario, who had been doing this for nearly twenty years, now came forward to meet us. His eyesight was failing, and his hands and feet were very much crippled by the disease. He had been dictating something

*Doña M.*

to another man, who was writing on a small table on the veranda, though his fingers also were affected and he wrote with difficulty. Both were very pleased to see us. I told Apolinario that Maria had often talked of the group there and had told of the little bitter orange tree, which they used as a Christmas tree by sticking candles in the little green fruit. "Oh," said Apolinario, "we can't do that now—it is too big, but it is still serving us as our shade tree there." I had not noticed that the umbrella tree was a bitter orange tree.

"We used to have a house of worship," he continued. "It was not always just like this. Look, those stones there are the remains of our meeting house. We keep them in memory of the fine pastors and preachers from North America and from South America who used to come and visit us and help us. It was a North American pastor who got the nice new hospital *pabellones* put up for us, but now bit by bit the people they employed here have all gone. Just recently the last one, Johannes Wirtz, had to go. He ran the cooperative, and it is a great loss."

Several had gathered by now on Apolinario's veranda. They were all very pleased to see Maria. The talk passed on to some of the difficulties Protestants meet. The carrying round of images was mentioned. One man said, "I've often watched the folk with their eyes riveted to the gold on the image. They are poor folk, but they would never think of stealing it; they think it is sacrosanct. I often think it would be better sold to feed the poor."

One of the women asked Maria to come and see her house, and Maria asked me, so I went with them and left Peter talking on the veranda. It was the usual Paraguayan campesino style. The only thing I found unusual was that the cow and the pig and the hens were as tame as the cat. Maria had often told me that folk with leprosy treat their animals like friends, because they can never have a child of their own about their doorsteps. If any babies are born, they are sent to the preventorium (a home where children liable to develop disease receive preventive care) in Asuncion, and the mother gets a photo of it each year.

We went back to Apolinario's. Peter had arranged that we try and find some way of sending them clothes and footwear, which they say they need very badly. As we left, I took a final look at the group on Apolinario's veranda. Some were very, very ragged indeed. And I remembered what Maria had told me—that those who met there did not come to look at each others' clothes, the way she had heard it often happens in churches.

On the way back to Maria's we saw a well-dressed man. I asked Maria who he was, and she said he was a German patient. Peter spoke to him in German. He was delighted to hear his mother tongue, and when he heard Maria was making final arrangements with her property at the colony, he said he wanted to buy her cow and would come in the morning to her house for it. He had altered his name to a Spanish form, so was known as Don Federico.

This was to be Maria's last night in the colony, and she had decided to have a little feast with the small group who eat at the Valenzuelas' house. She had given her last two or three hens to be cooked for it, as her contribution. She was busy cleaning out cupboards in her house, with many interruptions from visitors, so we left her and went back to the soldiers' *galpón*.

As we were on the way, we saw a youngish-looking man coming toward us. I remarked what a sad face he had. After he had passed us, he stopped and called to us in German. We said we had come with Doña Maria. He at once said he wished he had known before and that he would have come and met us earlier. I asked him his name, and when he said "Eugenio Kaiser," I at once placed him as the man, who with his *compañera* ("common-law wife"), had offered Maria a home when she arrived. She had broken down and said she just could not live in the *vieja sala* ("old dormitory") with all the women without fingers or noses, and this couple had come to the rescue. I told Eugenio how kind they had been to Maria on her arrival. "Oh, that was nothing. The beginning is a very hard time for everyone." He was sorry to hear we were leaving and said he would meet us at Maria's in the morning.

Next day (Tuesday) we set off early for the colony. Peter had been given the name of a man who has a wagon, and he set off to see if he could hire it for our journey to the station. We decided that I should call at the nuns' and give our permits in and then go to Maria's. I met a very pleasant, stout nun. She asked very warmly about Maria and said she was so glad to see her looking so well. I am sure she treats her patients with great love and devotion. Later at Maria's (when I said so) they all agreed that the nuns were not *cobardes* ("cowards"); they never thought of themselves when they were dressing terrible sores, but some were a bit fanatical about their religion—that was the trouble with some of them.

On the way to Maria's I heard someone call "Primavera." I looked round and saw a tall man with a farmworker's straw hat on his head. I did not recognize him. He spoke in good German and said, "I am Eugenio; I met you last night and said I would come to Maria's this morning." Then I realized that the hat altered his appearance very much. When we had spoken to him last night, he was bareheaded, with masses of black curling hair. We passed a few men standing at their doors, and he spoke in rapid Guaraní to them. Then he said to me, "My father was a German, and my mother was a *hiesige* [German for 'native']."

A few yards on we came to Maria's house. Eugenio was very glad to see Maria. They talked in Spanish, as Spanish is now Maria's chief language, after a disuse of German for eighteen years. Mauricio and Candido, Marina and José Valenzuela, and Don Federico were all there.

We were all sitting on tree stumps in front of Maria's veranda. Maria was busy inside packing. She then called to Mauricio, "Did you see where I put that money I had last night?" Mauricio arose and went in to help her search. He was more worried than she was over it. (Maria found it later when we arrived in Primavera—tied in a handkerchief.) It was the money Dorotea had given her for the clothes chest.

Don Federico had come to buy Maria's cow and to talk to us because we came from the outside world. He did not belong to Maria's circle of friends as the others did. Maria's friends were all either Protestants like Candido or honest haters of hypocrisy and superstition like Mauricio. Don Federico was a well-educated man with an intellectual bent. He said to me, "I expect you read Spanish? Have you read any good contemporary authors?"

"Only *La Rebelión de las Masas* ['The Rebellion of the Masses'] by Ortega y Gasset," said I.

Don Federico: Did you know he died this year? I liked some of his ideas. He said he liked the journey better than the destination. He knew it leads to tyranny when men claim to have reached their destination. Then they force other people to accept it too.

He was against all tyranny and said it was illogical to guillotine a prince and replace him with a principle. "That's what happens in totalitarianism."

He seemed to have kept abreast of the leprosy literature of the world, so far as he could get it. He knew all about the National Leprosarium in Carville, Louisiana. He said, "I try to keep in touch by reading and the radio. If I had money, I could get out, but as it is I can't, and I live in fear that any of my children may come here as patients. Better never see them than that."

At this point Peter returned, having fixed up a wagon for us. Don Federico asked him what he thought of the Eastern and Western blocks. "Oh," said Candido, "they are both rotten. The East preaches equality, but men are just used to produce material wealth for the state, and the West preaches democracy, but one man uses his fellows as a ladder to climb to wealth and success."

"That is why we try a third way," interjected Peter. "Yes," said Candido, "yours is the true communism. It can only come about in Christian love and brotherhood."

"The only brotherhood we have here is brotherhood in the disease," said Eugenio.

"It may look like a little paradise here," said Candido, "but in reality it is a little hell. People may appear happy, but it is only superficial."

"Yes," said Eugenio. "The folk have a kind of pride and shout '*Viva fulano* ["long live so-and-so"]!' when it is *fulano's* birthday, but deep down they may be feeling very unhappy."

Candido: They say no people are so quarrelsome as those with our disease.

Eugenio: It is egotism that is the trouble.

Candido: They all want material things, and materialism is a poison.

Eugenio: Now it is worse than ever, for the co-op is closed. We need work to keep our minds steady. Work keeps us happy as well as bringing in some necessary money.

Candido: But Don J. [Johannes Wirtz] had to go, and the co-op closed. It is always the same in the world. Jesus Christ spoke against falsehood, and he had to go to the Cross, and Don J. spoke against it, and he was thrown out.

Just then Mauricio, who was still helping Maria look for the money, found an old pair of shoes. He at first hailed them as a find. (Footwear is very, very scarce among them, and most people have sores or disintegrating toes, which should be protected from the mud.) Then Mauricio saw they were held together with wire, and he threw them away and said, "Those are Pablo's old, broken shoes."

Pablo Berg, the "prophet," had been looking after Maria's house in her absence. He was so advanced in the disease that he could not work. His only qualification was that he was honest, so he used to get caretaking jobs. He had died during Maria's absence and had passed the key of her house to Mauricio, as they were carrying him on the stretcher to the hospital.

I said, "I would have liked so much to meet him." "Yes," said Eugenio, "he was a real character. Folk said he had a screw loose, but he saw through things more clearly than most people, and he was fearless in saying it. He used to tell folk they had too much business interest mixed in with their religion, and he told the priest his flock were mostly goats— not sheep."

"Yes," said Marina Valenzuela, "he spoke straight at the rich and bossy, but he never refused to do a service to a poor person. He would go and stick up for them."

"His clothes were just rags," said José, "and his shoes were held together by wire, but he used to say he lacked nothing and that he felt fine."

"That is because he said the angels were with him," put in Maria.

"It was sad he advanced so fast in the disease," said Eugenio. "He was all right to look at a few years ago. Some folk just get quickly worse and worse, and others at the same stage and getting the same treatment get better just as quickly. I don't believe all the stuff they write in books. I see it disproved in life. They say young children are most likely to catch the contagion and must be kept away from it, yet we have quite a few young women here who were born and bred of diseased parents in the colony in the days before there was a preventorium, and now they are

married to patients, but they are all still fit and healthy. If you are fated
to catch the contagion, you will catch it."

Maria then shouted to me to ask me if I thought the bundle of rose
cuttings she had gathered together was too big. Marina Valenzuela was
helping her to cut them and tie them in a bit of sacking. "Oh no," I said.
"It is nice to take plenty, so that you have more chance that some will take
root."

Just then the wagon drew up to the stile, and we started taking leave.
Candido said, "It would be nice if you could be a kind of *madre dolorosa*
['grieving mother' as applied to Mother Mary] for us." "What is that,
Maria?" I asked, and she answered, "He wonders if you could take on
some of their needs, just the way a mother would." We asked them what
they most lacked, and they said footwear, underwear, and white rags for
bandages—or indeed any clothing. We said we would see what we could
arrange. I noticed both Mauricio and Candido had newspaper wrapped
round their feet in their shoes.

Mauricio accompanied us right to the administration house, as he had
to leave a stamped paper saying that Maria left him as agent for her house.
He walked without limping, and yet Maria had told me how bad his feet
were with ulcers and how, when he had no bandages, he would scoop the
mud out of his wounds with his penknife, till the blood ran. He did not
tell us anything about that; it was just part of the courage life demanded
of him.

The owner of our oxen wagon was a patient, who employs as driver a
healthy man living in the colony and shares with him the money thus
earned. I asked Maria why this young man, who scarcely knew a word of
Spanish, lived in the colony if he was healthy. "Oh, he has no possibility
of life outside. He was a patient here for a short time and was discharged
cured. But no one will believe he is free of contagion; he is avoided and
can't get work. He has tried it and come back to the colony."

On our return to Primavera Maria and I had a narrow escape, when the
riverboat bringing us from Asuncion to Puerto Rosario caught fire in
midstream during the night.

At 1 a.m. I wakened up with a strange feeling of choking in my throat.
The cabin was full of peculiar fumes. I felt I just *must* get some fresh air,
or I would suffocate. I slid down from my top bunk and put on my shoes,
and that wakened Maria in the bottom bunk. She said in a loud voice,
"Have we arrived at Rosario?" I said, "I must have some air. Don't you

D.P.

smell the fumes?" I opened the door and was taking in deep breaths when Maria cried out, "Fire! Fire!" I turned round, and sure enough the paintwork of the cabin had just caught on fire. It had been so hot it had been fuming and now caught fire. I said to Maria, "Come out and put on your shoes," and I wakened the men next door shouting, "*Fuego! Peligro!*" ("Fire! Danger!") as I helped Maria on with her shoes. Then I took her below deck, and all along the passage we wakened the people in their cabins. I left Maria down below and went up again to rescue our luggage. Maria said, "I could swim better without my boots." I said, "We may not need to do that."

The sailors had taken everything out onto the deck and were getting water out of the river in buckets and throwing it on our cabin wall, also in the next cabin. (These were the two hindmost cabins on the deck.) The top mattresses in each of these cabins were burnt. The men had fled barefoot, and the shoes they had left were shrunk to half size. It was only now I noticed that the boat had turned at right angles and was making for the shore. We stayed there for about an hour with the sailors throwing water on the walls of the two back cabins. Then we were told we could go back into our cabin again, but the doors of the two back cabins were fixed wide open, and a sailor came with a flashlight to inspect them every quarter hour.

I was dozing off to sleep when Maria said she saw sparks. I looked, and quite definitely we saw some big sparks. I went and called the sailor, and he tore down some charred paneling, which reached from floor to ceiling. It crumbled in his hands and broke in black fragments on the floor. Then we saw the cause of the trouble—a chimney with asbestos wound partly round it, leaving bare patches, which were very hot. The rest of the night I curled up on our luggage on the deck outside our cabin, so as to keep watch on it, and Maria went to sleep in her bunk.

My visit to the leper colony taught me a lesson in courage and faith. I was reminded of Dostoyevsky's saying that he had found "lovely goodness amid the utmost degradation and despair." Perhaps it takes hard times to call out these qualities in stronger measure, just as it takes a furnace to refine gold.

Doña M.

Doña M.

*Doña Maria's drawings illustrate the life that was around her in Paraguay.*

Doña M.

Doña M.

*Maria's memory, at 86 years of age, of her girlhood home.*

# Part 2

## IF I MAKE MY BED IN HELL, THOU ART THERE
(Ps. 139:8)

**Doña Maria's Life and Experiences,
Especially in the Santa Isabel Colony (1936-1954),
as Told by Herself to Maureen Burn**

# Chapter 1: LIFE IN ARGENTINA AND PARAGUAY

## From Bavaria to Argentina

I was brought to South America when I was five years old. We were a big Roman Catholic family, with a lot of boys. I was one of the youngest children. We came from Bavaria, where my father had a small cobbler's shop. He was a good cobbler but not a good businessman. He wanted to emigrate from Europe with all its wars and rumors of wars, especially as he had many sons.

So he was very excited when he read an advertisement of a big tract of land in Argentina, for a very small price. The neighbors reminded him that he knew nothing about agriculture, but he said that didn't matter, as he was just going to rear beef cattle on the land.

I remember the sea voyage. It seemed very long to me, and each day you could see nothing but the sea around you. I remember asking my mother if it would always be like that now, with nothing but the sea.

## Growing up in Argentina and Paraguay

When we got to Argentina, it seemed to me that instead of the sea we had nothing but flat prairie and grass around us.

My father had a big shock when he got to the big piece of land that he had bought, for he found that any water on it was salty, so it was useless for cattle. And he had sold up everything he had to buy it. So my father had to seek employment with a cattle rancher, and my big brothers became gauchos or cowboys.

My mother worked both indoors and out of doors, from dawn till dusk. She baked all the bread we ate and bought big rolls of cloth and made the dresses and shirts for us all. She used to get angry when she saw my father

26

give a titbit to a dog, and sometimes she would say, "I believe you would put that dog in one of the children's beds!"

The cattle ranch had wild beef cattle on it, and we children were warned not to go out among them. But one day three of us went out on the prairie to look for mushrooms. We thought it was all right, as the only cattle we saw were specks in the distance. Franz, my older brother, took charge of us. He must have been about seven years old then. We were so interested in looking for mushrooms and collecting a nice pile to take home, that we quite forgot the cattle.

Then suddenly Franz said, "Lie flat and don't breathe." A ring of wild cattle were coming nearer and nearer toward us. You could hear the thud of their hoofs, as we were lying flat against the earth, with one ear against the ground. Then you could also hear the cattle breathe.

I remember our father telling us to pretend to be dead, if wild cattle came near. I tried not to breathe at all. The cattle must have stopped coming any nearer, for I heard no more hoof thuds but only long-drawn-out sniffs and snorts of hot breath. We lay like this for a very long time—then they went away.

*Doña M.*

Another thing I remember about Argentina was the locusts. We used to think the "hoppers" were just like soldiers marching. They used to cast their coats two or three times, as they grew out of them, and we used to collect them off the grass stems.

I went to school for two years in Argentina. It was in Spanish; my parents only talked in German. I was much more interested in animals and living things than in book learning. I often would play truant, and the schoolteacher did not have much hope of teaching me anything. I used to beg my mother to let me stay at home and help with the outdoor work, which she found increasingly difficult, for her leg veins began to give her more and more trouble.

My parents were still undecided about whether I should leave school or not, when my father heard of cheap land further north in Paraguay, in a colony at one time settled by immigrants from Europe. When he had made sure the water there was fresh, not salt, we moved, leaving all the bigger boys in Argentina, where they found jobs and possibilities. That was the end of my schooling. I was then seven years old. I had had two years' schooling in Argentina and could read words of two or three letters, but I could not write or do figures. Anyway, I was very glad in later life that I could at least read a little.

We now had a little *chacra* or smallholding of our own, and I enjoyed helping my parents to work it. They knew I disliked school and loved animals, so they gladly accepted my help and gave me more and more responsibility. Years passed, and when my father was not making a success of his agricultural work, I used to take jobs away from home to earn some money, which I sent home for my parents. I went into domestic service in Asuncion or worked for a time in a corned beef factory. I always gladly returned home. I enjoyed meeting other young people and especially enjoyed the Saturday night dances, and I always wanted to be the "belle of the ball." But I noticed how many jealous brawls happened at these dances, and I didn't like that.

**First Contact With the Bible**

There was just one family of girls who were different. I got interested in them and asked them how it was that they were able to steer clear of all the jealousies and quarrels. They said they would ask me to their house one day when they had a visitor they were expecting.

When the day came, I went, and the visitor was a young man full of fire and eagerness to share something with us, which he called a "treasure." It was the Bible. He gave me one, and I decided I would try and read it. But I found it was much too difficult to read and that I would have to practice reading.

When my parents saw me spelling out the words and figuring out—better and better as time went by—what word the letters stood for, they said, "Whatever are you doing that for? Religion is just for real sinners." But that did not put me off from trying to understand what was written. And I always went to this Protestant family, when someone came there to explain the Bible.

There were many things I could not understand in the beliefs of these people. They used to speak against "images" and call it idolatry. But we in our family had always admired something our nearest neighbor had, and I often used to make an excuse to go to their house so that I could have another look at it. It was a figure of the Virgin dressed in red and blue, with golden borders to her draperies and a golden halo. Many people living in that district also admired this figure. The old lady in the house had brought it with her from Europe many years ago, and the daughter was always afraid someone would steal it. So when the old lady died, the daughter put it in the coffin by the side of her mother, and it was buried with her.

Years passed, and I continued to learn more about the Bible, when someone came to explain it. Often it was someone from the Salvation Army who came. My father also started coming, and a few more local people began to come too.

## Marriage

Among them was the man I later married. His name was Adolf, and he had a *chacra* not far away. His parents, like mine, had come out from Europe. The year after we married, we had a little son. He was fair with blue eyes and had the loveliest nature any child could ever have.

Life was very happy. Adolf did the arable work on our *chacra*, and I looked after the animals and birds. We each did our favorite kind of work on the *chacra*, and our little son kept running from one to the other, and we didn't have a care in the world.

*Doña M.*

# Chapter 2: TO THE LEPER COLONY

## In Isolation at Home

Our happiness only lasted for five or six years. Then one day Adolf asked me how I had burnt myself, and he pointed to a big blister on the back of my arm. I had not noticed it, and I could not feel it. This happened two or three times. I spilled boiling water on my feet, when pouring it off the pig food. I felt nothing and only later noticed the blister. Adolf got worried and took me to the doctor. The doctor took tests of skin and blood and sent them away to be examined. But the answers all came back saying nothing had been found.

In spite of this, the doctor said it would be safer if I lived apart, until we knew what was the matter with me. Adolf built a little house on our land, and I moved in, and every now and then I had more tests taken and sent away, but the answers all came back saying nothing had been found.

For two years I lived alone like this, or tried to live alone, for my little son used to keep running to me to ask me to come and look at something, or to come and see what he was making or doing. It about broke my heart to have to send him away.

Once I went with him. He had made a little trench and put pieces of glowing wood in it. He had got the glowing wood out of the fire on a shovel and put it in the trench and covered it over with earth, and he said he was making charcoal for my brazier. I knew he must have been watching the men making charcoal. I was so proud of his getting the hang of the charcoal making, and he only seven years old, and he was pleased I had come. But the doctor was really angry and said I must keep away from the child.

So I could do nothing for my husband and child, except keep away. The only thing I could do was to collect my own firewood. I used to go far into the forest collecting fallen branches and often had a big bundle of firewood to bring home. Many a time I would startle a big rattlesnake or a *yararé acá curusú* (Bothrops snake) under the fallen branches. But I just could not be afraid of them, for I was facing something much worse than a snake bite—the fear of being sent away to the leper colony.

I often wondered if all the loneliness of my isolation and the sorrow of seeing my family neglected in many ways was necessary, as my tests always came back with nothing found in them. It was this kind of uncertainty that was the hardest to bear.

People all avoided me because of fear of the disease. I just had no heart to cook or eat anything, and I got as thin as a rake because of grief. I did not know anyone could live and be so skinny. I then took ill, but it was more the illness of sorrow than anything else. If I had found a pile of gold in those days, it would not have interested me. I saw everything with the eyes of my grief, and everything looked strange and different. I used to wonder if the sun would rise again next morning in this terrible world of grief I was in.

**Sorrowful Journey**

We decided we could not go on much longer like this. So Adolf took me to a big doctor in the capital city, and my sister-in-law kept the child. We wanted to know, one way or the other, about my illness. The big doctor took a look at my arms and legs and stuck pins in and did other tests to see how much I could feel. Then he said I had leprosy and that I should go to the leper colony and get treatment, and perhaps I would get no worse.

So we made arrangements to go as soon as we could after returning home. My sister-in-law continued to keep the boy for us, and Adolf said I should think of all the things I would need. But I had no interest in anything. So he got together my clothes and a few old photos I had of my parents and my brothers and sisters. He also said I should take cooking pots and bedding, and he said he would like me to take the fine eiderdown my mother had made for me when I married.

Then he ordered a wagoner to take us, and he came with me the four days' journey to the leper colony. It felt to me like going into the grave, that journey did. My heart was frozen with grief, and I could not think. We did not speak—there were no words suitable. When we reached the gates of the colony, the wagoner spoke to the man there, and he was told to pull up at the women's *sala* ("dormitory"). This was a very rough, old building, more like a *galpón* ("barn" or "shed").

I did not know at the time that it was where the more advanced cases were housed. So I got such a shock when a lot of women crowded out to see who had come. Some had no noses, some had no fingers, some had feet like horses' hoofs, because they had lost their toes, and many of them had faces that looked alike, because they had no eyebrows.

I was so frightened to see this all of a sudden that I burst into tears and told Adolf I just could not live among them. More and more people were collecting round us and looking at us and the things Adolf had brought. They were speaking in a dialect we couldn't understand. Poor Adolf did not know what to do, and the wagoner wanted to unload.

**Eugenio and Anastasia**

Then a man pushed through the crowd and spoke in German. He had guessed we were gringos (foreigners), because we were fair. He seemed to understand all that we were feeling, and we did not need to explain. He talked to Adolf and then took us to his house and said I could stay with them as long as I liked and until I had found my feet in the colony.

We also met the woman of the house. Neither of these two were frightening to look at. They looked no different from people outside the colony. This was a comfort to us both after the shock we had had. The woman said it was always very hard for a new patient at the beginning and that they had all been through it, and she repeated what the man had said about me being welcome to stay as long as I wished.

Then Adolf and I had to part. I will never forget the wagon disappearing into the distance, taking him away from me. It was all I could do to stop myself running after it. I stood and watched it out of sight and felt more dead than alive.

Then someone took my arm. It was Anastasia, the woman of the house. I had not noticed her till then. She must have been there all the time. She took me home and got a bed ready for me on the wide veranda, as they had only one room, which they occupied.

I lay down just as I was without taking off my clothes and did not even think of thanking her. She did not mind and left me alone, except for bringing me some food, but I could not eat it. Eugenio, the man, was also kind and did not bother me with talk. I lay there wishing only to die and end it all.

But as evening came on, I was shocked and alarmed to find a stream of Eugenio's boon companions come with guitars and much singing and laughter. Those who had no seats came and sat on my bed. They must have decided I was asleep or crazy. I wondered what the respectable folk at home would have thought. Nothing unpleasant ever happened, but I made sure I was in bed every night before the crowd came, otherwise I could not get to bed till after they had gone.

## Chapter 3: FIRST YEARS IN THE LEPER COLONY

### A Time of Grief

After this, a long time passed, in which my only wish was to die and forget my misery. I had lost faith in everything. I believed neither in God nor the devil, and I never thought of the Bible anymore. I thought what good had it been—it hadn't saved me from all this. I had quite forgotten how to smile and was more like a log than a living person.

Anastasia was very kind to me. She brought me my food and never pressed me to do any work in return for it. She said I could help her with the work if I wished, but I didn't wish to do anything. I just sat there pining for my husband and child. I must have continued like this for a couple of years.

### Back to the Bible

Then one day when I was sitting out in the shade of a tree, a stranger came up to me and shook my hand and said, "How are you, Doña Maria?"

I wondered how he knew my name, so I looked at his face and recognized the keen young evangelist who had first told me about the Bible years before. His eyes were the same, though he was no longer so young.

I said, "I am very unhappy."

He said, "Seek for Jesus Christ," and he left me without another word.

I thought, "What a strange thing to say, and not a word of sympathy!" I went indoors and rooted out my Bible from the bottom of my *baúl* ("trunk"). I opened it and tried to read it but could not make head or tail of it. When Eugenio saw me with it, he said, "There is a group that reads

36

the Bible every Sunday morning. They are Protestants of all kinds, and anyone can go and ask them to explain it."

So I went. The group met at the *ranchito* ("hut") of a man called Apolinario. He welcomed me and told me I could come any time, and he gave me the present of a bombilla. He said I should learn to take yerba maté with it. It was a good *pasatiempo* ("pastime"), it was wholesome, and it would mix well with my thoughts about my husband and my son, and God.

And I found that to be true, and I began to go every Sunday to the *reunión* ("gathering"), and I began to understand bits of the Bible, the way Apolinario explained it. And then I began slowly to come alive again. I stopped sitting about, and I began to help Anastasia with her work.

Doña M.

## "Marriages" in the Colony

I noticed that Anastasia got into trouble with Eugenio, when he found out that she had men visitors. Sometimes he would beat her, and sometimes he would just refuse to eat with her. She did not mind being beaten; she thought it was a compliment, but she was terribly hurt if Eugenio just refused to eat with her.

One day after a big row with Eugenio, I ventured to say to Anastasia that it was her fault for making him jealous. But Anastasia said, "I can do as I like, for I'm not married to Eugenio. He can't marry, for he has a wife outside."

I was very surprised and asked where Eugenio's wife lived. "Eugenio doesn't know," she said. I was more surprised, till Anastasia explained that the wife was so scared when Eugenio took leprosy that she moved away and left no address, for she didn't want letters that might carry the infection, and she took the children with her. So Eugenio did not know where they were either.

I later found out that there were many folk in the colony who were in the same position as Eugenio. It was said of them that they were "married and yet not married"; so it was said there was a different marriage law in the colony from the one outside.

As I began to take interest in my surroundings and in the lives of those around me, I gradually began to find out a great deal about the lot of people who were already married when they took leprosy. It was not always as had happened with Eugenio. I found couples where the opposite had happened and the wife had accompanied her husband to the colony, when he had taken leprosy.

There were women in the colony who had lived fifteen or twenty years with severely ill husbands, without taking any precautions to protect themselves, and they had not taken the disease. When I first heard this, I was very surprised and asked how this could be, and I was told, "You won't get it if you are not afraid for your own skin!"

I also noticed that many very poor women living near the colony were only too glad to come and live as wives or *compañeras* to patients, for then they got an assured ration of food free. They were more afraid of hunger than of leprosy.

I also found that people in the colony were more afraid of tuberculosis than of leprosy. Tuberculosis was looked on as a killer. Most people, before coming to the colony, had known of cases where perhaps a whole family had died, one after the other, with tuberculosis. But people could live a lifetime with leprosy and then die of flu or jaundice or something else. I was told there was a beautiful house lying empty in the colony, for its last owner died of tuberculosis. No one would live in it, even though there was always a shortage of private houses in the colony.

### Apolinario

I did not learn all this at once but just bit by bit, as I began to forget my own sorrows and look around me. I went regularly to the *reunión* on Sunday morning, and I felt something strong and helpful in Apolinario. He was happy and had a trust in God, in spite of his very advanced stage of the disease. This interested me so I asked him to tell me the story of his life.

Apolinario had been a soldier in the Bolivia-Paraguay War (1932-1935). He was a devout Roman Catholic and practiced his religion conscientiously. He had seriously studied the Roman Catholic catechism, but he found something lacking. The thing he was looking for was a direct way to God without any priest or other man being necessary as a go-between. He was badly wounded and spent many months in hospital in Asuncion. A Salvation Army "lassie" used to come round the ward, visiting the patients and giving out Bibles to any who were interested. He took one and read it with deepening interest, for he thought it certainly spoke of a direct way to God, with Jesus the only mediator to show the way. He put a lot of questions to the lassie, and she said they believed the way he did. So Apolinario decided he wanted to put his life straight with God and with man. This caused him a bitter and painful struggle, which tore him for weeks, for he knew what the consequences would be if he confessed what he had been hiding. So he confessed that he had leprosy. It also meant that he marry his *compañera*, who was mother of his three children, all of whom he now had to leave and go to the newly opened leper colony at Sapucay.

**The True Teacher**

Ever since then (1936) Apolinario had been trying to pass on to others what he had found. He held a little group of Protestants together and helped many to find a new strength and overcoming of their sorrow through faith. This often meant teaching people to read, so that they could read the Bible. But he would always tell them, "A man can only teach another a little bit about the Bible. The true teacher is the Spirit of God in the believer's heart. He will show you the meaning more and more, as you trust Him more and more in your life. Then you will find the Bible is an endless treasure house—you will always get something new out of it that you did not see before. It will become a lamp to your feet."

*Doña M.*

**The Devil's Lasso Is Long**

After the meeting on Sunday morning at Apolinario's *ranchito* ("hut"), we used to have some fine talks. Apolinario was especially glad to welcome unbelievers. They often said they found no attraction in religion, as religious folk were often so sour-faced. "Oh," said Apolinario, "that is unfortunately true, but such people are not yet free of the hold of the devil." Some people were surprised when they heard this, but Apolinario continued, "Very few people realize that it is the good folk who are the devil's working-ground. He is kept busy working on them. He does not need to bother about folk who just live for their lusts. He has them already in his kingdom, and he can leave them in peace, as they don't know he exists. But as soon as a man begins to think, 'Perhaps there is a God,' then he begins to know there is a devil also. The man may think he is out of the devil's power, because he has stopped sinning, but as soon as he goes about in fear of the power of evil, he is still lassoed. Some good people are always on the lookout for evil and see evil possibilities in everything, so they frighten away the young with their sour looks. If only they knew how dangerous it is to think of the devil without each time thinking of God, to let your mind so dwell on evil that you forget that God is the stronger! The only way to cut free from the devil's lasso is to cut the bonds of fear, in faith in Christ's victory."

**God Is No Respecter of Persons**

Sometimes one or two of the stern and judging members of the *reunión* criticized Apolinario for welcoming "sinners," for he was always warmhearted and outgoing to such. Then he used to say, "You are judging them, but only God can judge correctly, because He alone can see everything in a man's heart." Or he would say, "You must have love instead of judgment in your heart. Nothing pleases the devil more than to get us to climb into the judgment seat and judge others."

Or again he would say, "Just look at the way Jesus treated the woman of Samaria at the well, and look at the way He treated Nicodemus. The Samaritan woman was living with a *compañero* and had had five *compañeros* before him, while Nicodemus was a good-living man, widely respected as a teacher and councilor among the devout Jews. Jesus knew all this, but nevertheless He offered the woman living water, and He told Nicodemus he must be born again. We would have done it the other way round, and Nicodemus would have been offered the living water, and the woman would have been told she must be born again. We judge by the outward appearance, but God sees into the heart. His eyes are not as our eyes, and His judgments are not as our judgments."

### God Dwells in the Heart That Forgives

There was a woman in the colony called Sara. She had to part from her husband when she took the disease, and she thought she would never see him again. She was very broken-down for the first years, and then she took a *compañero* called Justo, and they lived ten years or more together, but all the time Justo got worse and worse and more crippled, and Sara's health got better and better. In the end Justo died, and soon afterwards the doctor told Sara she was "symptom free" and could leave the colony. Sara wrote this news to her relatives, and the relatives wrote Sara that her husband was willing to have her back, even though he knew all about Justo. Then at the end of the letter they wrote that Sara's husband still called himself an agnostic. This worried Sara, because she had become very religious in the way of always attending mass and saints' days and saying her rosary very often.

I asked Apolinario what he thought about it, and he said, "There is no value in just believing in God. The devils do and tremble. And there is not much value in outward religious practices. It is the heart that matters and what is in the heart. If that husband is really forgiving from the heart, then something of God is in him, even though he says he is an agnostic, for no one can forgive without God."

### Thomas the Blind

Another day at Apolinario's we were talking about "doubting Thomas." Apolinario said, "The disciple Thomas was *un muy gran ciego* ['a very blind man']. His spiritual eyes were blind until they got proof from his bodily eyes and from his fingers. He had to see the risen Lord and touch His wounds before he would believe."

"Many people are like that," continued Apolinario. "They trust what their eyes and ears and senses tell them before they will believe what the inner eye and inner voice tell them. This is a great danger to Christians, and the Gospel warns us that people will point, 'Lo, there is Christ! Lo, here is Christ!' But we must not be misled. The eyes can be deceived by the outward appearance of holiness, whereas the Kingdom of Heaven is within you. That is where it is to be found and then lived by."

**The Proud Vultures**

Apolinario used to warn people against pride. He said it came in all kinds of ways to people, but that one of the worst ways was when it made people proud of their goodness. He used to tell a story about pride.

Long ago the vultures of Paraguay had beautiful voices, says an old legend. The campos (prairies) were full of their song, and people used to linger to listen to it. This puffed up the vultures, and they became very proud.

One day a big chief ordered all the birds of the campo and the forest and the river to come to a big fiesta. There would be plenty of good food of every type to suit each taste—seed and fruit and flesh and fish and frog and insects. There would be a big contest of song; the birds were to sing in turn, and a wonderful gift would be given to the winner.

The smaller birds at once looked for suitable perches on the trees, where they could practice their songs and improve them. Some practiced new notes to add to their songs. But the vultures kept silent. They did not want any of the smaller birds to copy any part of their song. They also did not think they needed any more practice, for they thought their song was perfect.

But the great chief knew what was in their hearts. He hated one thing, and that was pride. When the big day came for the festival, he punished them. When it was their turn to sing, the only voice they could summon up was the croak they have to this day.

*Doña M.*

**Jealousies in the Colony**

All this time I was still living with Eugenio and Anastasia, but now I began to want to be independent. However, *ranchitos* (small one-roomed dwellings) were scarce. I had already noticed that there were many quarrels over women throughout the colony, but I later saw that there were even more quarrels over the better-paid jobs.

Eugenio had a job like this; he was a foreman, and I noticed he was watched closely by a group of men, each of whom envied him his job. They were always on the lookout to pick on any fault to discredit him. There were often raised voices when they came to the house, and once the row grew to such proportions that the men drew out their machetes (bush knives).

I said to Eugenio afterwards, "You would find better protection in this than in your machete," and I pointed to the Bible. Eugenio laughed and said, "Yes, if I had faith, but I have none, so I have to protect myself as best I can." A week later he received a knife wound and had to go to hospital, and it was only six years later that he again had a foreman's job.


**In the "German"** *Ranchito*

How I became independent happened this way. Some of my friends from the *reunión* came and told me that now was my chance. An elderly German patient had died in a little *ranchito*, left by a previous German patient for the use of Germans. Only if no German applied, could it go to someone else.

I told Anastasia about it, but she did not want me to leave, and when I persisted, she was angry and said, "Well, if you go, don't ever try to come back again." In spite of that, she has always remained friendly and always kept asking me to come and visit.

As I was the only German without a house, I got it without difficulty, thanks to the generosity of a former German patient. No sooner had I moved in than I realized how kind and generous Eugenio and Anastasia had been. They had given me of their own home-produced milk and eggs, without charging me. I had thought till then that the milk and eggs were on the government food ration. So I decided to earn some money, so as to be able to buy such things. I decided to take in washing.

# Chapter 4: ASPECTS OF LIFE IN THE COLONY

## A Washerwoman's Life

I made inquiries from the women who took in washing. But I soon found that they had already booked up all the people who were richer and had more changes of clothing and did not do any dirty work.

I found I could only get the worst bundles, belonging to the poorest and most neglected. Often they belonged to men who "did" for themselves, instead of giving up their freedom and going into the men's *sala*. These bundles were refused by everyone else. They were so dirty you had to wash them two or three times before they became clean.

As soon as I had got together my bundles for washing, I went with the other women to the *arroyo* (brook) that flows through the colony. The *arroyo* has nice big, flat stones on its banks. The women wet the clothes in the flowing water, then spread them on the flat stones and soap them well. Then they spread the clothes on the grass, so that the sun can work on the soap. After that they rinse them out in the running water.

Some of the women had no fingers; their hands were just like cat's paws, so they just patted the clothes as best they could. When the clothes were washed, I would put them in a basket and carry them home. Then I dried them, ironed them, and mended them.

It was quite safe leaving clothes hanging on the line at the German cottage, for it was toward the center of the colony and well out of reach of the folk outside, who used to steal so much from the patients living near the boundary fence.

M.

45

*Doña M.*

## My Animals

I put my earnings together with some money my husband had sent me, and I was able to buy a pig and some hens, but I still wanted a cow. I worked very hard, but cows are very dear. Then I heard of one that was cheap, because she was very old. I was interested in her, because she was with calf. Folk told me she might die before the calf was born. Others said, "What if it is a bull calf? Your money will have been wasted." However, I risked it, and everyone laughed when they saw me bring the old cow home. They called her "a bag of bones."

I looked after the cow well, and she gave birth to a beautiful, glossy, black heifer calf. I called the calf "Mehi," and I would let it have all the milk, as I wanted it to have a good start in life.

Then one day the cow was missing. I searched all over the campo for her, and then a man on horseback told me he had seen her down a steep gully. I found her there, and she could not rise to her feet. So I took the calf home and came daily with alfalfa and maize husks and water for the cow. She died, and a neighbor helped me to skin her, and we made hide ropes and shared them.

Mehi, the calf, became as tame as a dog. I kept her in the house at night till she grew a bit bigger, and after that I only brought her in in the cold weather. During the day she was on the campo. I never needed to go out and fetch her from the campo, for she knew I always had some well-scrubbed mandioca peelings ready for her at home with plenty of salt rubbed in.

Cows need salt, and if they do not get it, they will chew the washing off the line to get the salt out of the soap. Other women often had their washing chewed, because they did not know this; they were usually women from the towns. Folk used to tell me they could set their clocks by listening for Mehi's "moo," as she turned the corner into my patio (yard) each evening.

Most of my life I have got up with the hens and gone to bed with the hens. Like the hens I could tell by the sun it was time to get up or go to bed. I could also tell the time, more or less, by the sun during the whole day, and that was good enough for me.

But I was always getting into trouble in the colony for not being on time. They used to tell me I had come too late for the doctor's consultation hour, or they would tell me I had come too early to get my provisions. I've never had a clock, and I can't read one. I never felt I needed one, just like the birds, which fly about freely and don't know anything about the exact time.

Getting up and going to bed with the sun was a good saving on candles, which are a very expensive kind of lighting. I later saved up and bought a lamp and found kerosene much cheaper, but I did not use it often—only when there was a noise in the night. Animals can often make quite a noise at night, especially if they are in the same room. I always used to bring in very young pigs and later on Mehi's calves, when the weather was frosty, and I never lost a young animal. I sold them when they were bigger, and then I could buy things I needed.

I also got a dog. It and the cat were both black like Mehi, and folk used to ask if I had especially chosen them all black. I would laugh and say, "No, they are just the way God sent them to me."

One night I wakened up, because my dog gave a lot of sharp yelps of pain. I groped about for a candle but couldn't find one. Then a neighbor came in and said he saw a small snake go out of the door. He left his lamp with me, and I tried to soothe the dog, but he died in an hour. When I took off my shoes, I found the candle had fallen into one shoe and I had crushed it by walking about on it. I had not felt it; that was my trouble: I had lost feeling in my hands and feet.

I was very upset about my dog. He was so *letrado* ("wise") that he knew any hen that was not mine, and he used to pick it out when it was eating with my hens and chase it away. He was also a good companion to me.

I tried to plant some vegetables and maize (corn), but soon gave it up as hopeless. Most people, like myself, could not afford to buy a fence, so everyone's pigs and hens wandered about freely and destroyed anything I had planted.

Another thing that I was sorry about was that no one buried a hen or chick that had died. So the cats and the pigs ate them and took such a fancy to poultry that they started to kill for their own use. Then all the cats had to be got rid of, but what can you do about a pig that wouldn't fatten because it was too saucy to eat pig food?

Sometimes our stores came in a bad condition with whiskers of mold on the *galletas* or with maggots in the beans or maize. Then I used to feed it all to my animals. But I always kept some good grain for a rainy day, when I couldn't go out. On a dry day, if my feet were not troubling me, I used to go out with a sack and collect *planta del chancho* ("sow thistle")

for my pig. I was often so eager to fill my sack that I wandered far before
I noticed I had lost a shoe. Then I would have to go back to find it.


## Foot Troubles Among the Patients

This kind of thing often happens, as most folk with leprosy have lost
the sense of feeling in their feet. Often when the young folk are dancing,
someone shouts to a young girl that her shoe is off. And when the kindly
old priest, Padre Ochoa, comes to visit the colony, he follows up his usual
greeting, *"Que Dios le bendiga* ['God bless you']!" with *"Cómo andan
sus patitas* ['How are your little paws']?" There is no need to worry about
shoe fashions in the colony—so many folk go about with one shoe and
one slipper. You can even save shoe leather by wearing out odd bits of
footwear, and no one will notice. Before I took the disease, I was able to
work in my bare feet on our smallholding at home, but after that the soil
seemed to irritate my feet, so I had to use footwear.

*Alpargatas* were cheap. They were rope-soled canvas shoes, but they
did not last long. Also I found soil came in through the soles, so I used
to save on clothes and buy boots. When gifts were being given out, I
always hoped I might get some leather boots, but mostly they were dainty
town styles, which would not go on my feet. So I had to save up money
to buy leather boots, while my clothes were very faded and shabby. The
women washing clothes down by the river used to look me up and down
and say, "Doña Maria, why don't you sell your calf and buy yourself a
new rig-out?"


## The Babes and the Wise

I often think that I have had little more education than my hens. I had
a little schooling but never got beyond the first grade. My mother got a
bad leg after my youngest sister was born, so I was needed to help at
home and on our little *chacra*. I was only too glad to leave school; I liked
animals much better. I learnt to read slowly after I left school, but I never
learnt to write or to do figures. I always had to ask other people to write
for me. Usually they ask pay for it, but I always had someone among my
friends who could write and who did it as a little service for me.

Some folk were very ashamed to admit they could not write. But I used to think, "If you can't write, it keeps you from being proud of yourself." And I remembered that it says in the Bible, "God visits the humble and resists the proud."

Learning is a good thing unless it makes you proud, and living a good life is a good thing unless it makes you proud of your goodness.

It also says in the Bible that the truth is revealed to babes but hidden from the wise. But God is not bound by rules, just as you can see among the disciples. They say some of them could not read or write, but others were quite learned.

### Ill in the "Old Hall"

One day I took ill and had to be taken to the *vieja sala*. A neighbor arranged for a man to look after my animals for pay, but I did not have time to tell him about Mehi's mandioca peelings with salt rubbed in.

This *vieja sala* was the old hospital, where the wagon drew up when I first arrived. It was not much more than a big *galpón*. People would do as they liked in it. They would put their beds where they liked and could sweep, or not sweep, their part of the floor, and those who had charcoal braziers put them just where they liked. The floor was beaten earth, so cinders falling from the brazier did not do it any harm.

The women used to go out and make themselves brooms from brushwood or stringy weeds to sweep up the ash from the braziers. But rows used to start, and it was always the "houseproud" women who started them. They would not just keep to their own bit of floor space but would come and look under the beds of the other patients and tell them they hadn't swept under the bed.

**Dust Unto Dust**

This reminded me how years ago, when I was a young girl, I worked for a time in a big house in Asuncion. There were two of us to do the work for the family. The mistress was very particular and checked everything we did, whether it was washing clothes or housework. If she found the smallest spot on a bedcover we had washed and ironed, she said, "Wash it again and use soap and a brush on that spot." Or if she found a table leg not dusted or a china dog ornament with dust in its ears, she would not be content till all dust had been removed.

The whole house had to be polished like a mirror, and the children were not able to play freely in case they left finger marks on the furniture. All this checking up kept the mistress on the go all the time, so she hardly rested in the siesta and was thin and worn because of it.

So when I now looked at the *ranchitos* of my neighbors in the colony and my own *ranchito*, where no one had time to dust, I used to think of that mistress. And I would think: Surely it must have been a kind of pride in that woman, which made her think she was so superior to a bit of dust. So she spent her life seeing that there was no dust in the same room as herself. She had forgotten that she was made out of dust and would one day return to dust, unless she looked to higher things.

Our meals in the *vieja sala* were brought in in the large cooking pot in which it had been cooked. The pot was put on the table, and we came and helped ourselves out of it. It was usually polenta (cornmeal mush) or *puchero* ("meat and vegetable stew").

My neighbors used to come and visit me and told me the man at my house never gave Mehi any mandioca peelings and that Mehi was always looking for me. One day when I was up a bit and sat by the window talking to some other patients, Mehi must have heard my voice, for she came round and put her head right in through the window. It was the old campesino (countryman's) type of window, with no glass panes and only boards, which could fit one on the top of the other to act as a shutter on a cold night.

Doña M.

## Life With Felipa

While I was still in the *vieja sala*, I got news that the German cottage could no longer be had free of rent. As I could not pay what was asked, I had to inquire about other accommodation. A woman in the *vieja sala* asked me to come and live with her and help her with her work and with her two children, Julio, aged eight, and Braulia, aged six. The woman's name was Felipa.

So I went to live with her. The children had beautiful toys, sent by charities or religious groups outside. Braulia had beautiful dolls, the like of which I had never seen. Julio also had toys, but he never played with them. The only thing that interested him was his guitar. He could play any songs on it by ear. He used to listen to the serenades being played and sung, and he could play *"Al pie de tu ventana* ['Beneath your window']" as well as any grown-up guitarist. That was the commonest serenading song. But he longed to have a harp also. Many years later, when he was a man, Julio made his living by his harp playing.

My time with Felipa was not easy, for it made her angry to see me read the Bible. She thought I was proud to think I could understand a book that only the priests could understand. She used to try and frighten me out of reading it by saying there was a law coming out that heretics were to be drowned. I did not know if it were true or not, but I didn't give up reading the Bible.

## My New *Ranchito*

Then I heard of a house that was cheap, as it was in such bad repair. I got a letter writer to write and ask my husband if he could help me buy it, which he did. The disadvantage of this house was that it was near the boundary, so I found I was robbed of anything I left lying about outside. I lost my cooking pot, and I even lost my big feather eiderdown, which I had brought with me from home. I had hung it on my line to air in the sunshine.

But one good thing was that I was near a wood and could collect a nice, big pile of firewood. I used to take my axe and go out for the day or just for the morning. But one day I was so pleased with myself for chopping such a nice pile of wood that I forgot to bring my axe home with me. That

was a big loss; I asked a man living nearby if he had seen it. He said,
"What will you give me if I find it for you?"

Often you heard people say, *"Nadie hace ni un pelo sin dinero* ['No
one will do the least bit without pay']." This was said about the rich as
well as about the poor. I was once collecting sow thistle outside the patio
of a very fine house. The owner came out and said, "How much will you
pay me for that?" But I went off and left her with her sow thistle weeds,
which she could not use herself, as she had no pig.

### The Squashed Pumpkins, or the Root of War

One day in the meat queue the folk were laughing about Don
Federico's latest joke. Don Federico was very learned. He had lots of
newspapers sent to him, because he wanted to know all that was
happening in the world. For the past months his whole talk had been
about the atom bomb, which he said was a terrible and crazy thing. Now
he had said that if an atom bomb were to fall on the colony, it would be
a blessing—everyone would be cured in a flash!

Candido, a student, was standing next to me in the queue. He
sometimes came to Apolinario's. I turned to him and said, "I am a *tonta*
("stupid person"). I can't figure out what an atom bomb is like." "You
don't need to figure it out," he said. "It is just what happens when you
have bigger and better wars. But the root of all wars is the same—greed
and envy."

I thought about that. I didn't know anything about war, but I knew
plenty about greed and envy, not only in rich people but in very poor
people.

The man from whom I had bought my house had been a poor man and
unable to do any repairs. I could understand that, but I could not
understand why he had slashed and cut anything he could not uproot and
take with him. He had even cut down two lovely creepers by the patio,
because they would not transplant. They were lying on the ground
withered. One was a beautiful mauve passion flower in bloom, and the
other was *Sábado tarde* ("Saturday afternoon"), which has a beautiful
scent and is used instead of perfume, though the flowers are greenish and
not beautiful.

However, the creepers both began to grow again and made a nice bit of shade for my patio, and such a beautiful scent from the *Sábado tarde!* So I was very glad.

Another time I saw a man move to another house in the colony, and he went round squashing all his ripening pumpkins. I could not understand, so I asked him why he was wasting them like that.

"Oh," he said, "they won't ripen if I pick them and take them with me; they're too green yet."

"But why don't you leave them for the next man who will be living there?"

"I don't want another man to gain by my labors," said he. "I planted them, I looked after them and watered them."

"Well," said I, "what about all the hungry pigs that wander around looking for something to eat? Couldn't you have left the pumpkins for them?"

"I don't want another man's pigs to fatten on my labor," said he. So we said no more about it.

That spirit is the root of war. It is very strong, but God is stronger.

*Doña M.*

**Courage Spiced With Humor**

But everyone has a good side to his nature, and there was very much that was fine in the folk around me, like the courage they showed in their disease and the sense of humor they showed, sometimes even having a laugh at the disease itself. I used to hear many a laugh as we stood in the long queue waiting for our stores.

One day a couple of men who work for STICA told of how they had come upon a big rattlesnake just a foot away from them. Several exclaimed how lucky they were that it hadn't struck. Someone said, "It's strange that no one has ever been bitten in the colony, though we quite often come across snakes."

"It's not strange at all," said another. "The snakes don't bite us because they don't want to become *leprosos* ('lepers')."

When the laughter had died down, someone added more seriously, "I've heard it said that snakes and other *bichos* ('little animals, vermin') keep away from us because they don't like the smell of sulphur from our sulfa drugs."

Another day, in the queue for meat a man had just been given his lump of meat, and straightaway he let it slip out of his hands into the mud, because he could not feel it. Then he laughed and said "*Leproso* ['leper']!"

Yet another day there was a good laugh over the quality of the *galletas* that were being given out. They had whiskers of mold on them. They were of no use except as hen food but were nevertheless received with a lot of laughter, and speculation about who got the profits of palming the moldy *galletas* off onto the colony—perhaps some merchant and some commissary had put their heads together and shared the profits. So usually there was a cheerful atmosphere of banter in the queue.

### The Healthy Ones in the Colony

But it was very different when gifts were being given out and when crippled patients arrived at the end of the queue, to find that the *sanas* ("healthy women") had run there first and taken the pick of the lot. This was one of the main reasons why *sanas* were not liked, and those who wanted them banished from the colony based their argument on this. But there are many more men than women among the four hundred patients, and the majority of patients voted for keeping the colony open to the eighty or so *sanas*, so that they could become wives or *compañeras* to patients who lived alone and were getting a bit too crippled to "do" for themselves. But the *sanas* did cause a lot of trouble and jealousy in the colony; they would take what they could from a patient and then leave him. That is why some men said they would never have a *sana* but would prefer to have one of the women patients as wife or *compañera*. They said you could never be sure of a *sana*, for she was free to go out and visit the villages or the capital, but a patient was always there in the colony.

There were also a few healthy men (*sanos*) in the colony. They are often given jobs like wagon driving out of the colony to collect provisions or parcels. They lived in the colony because they all had a similar story to one I heard of from a woman with whom I washed clothes. This woman said she had been very surprised to see a young man from her home village arrive a couple of years ago. The lad had been told by his doctor that his disease had been diagnosed early, so there was every hope that he would be out of the colony soon. He had just been about a year in the colony when he was told he could go. He was nearly beside himself with joy and could hardly wait to go home. He was thinking of his girl.

His mother welcomed him under her roof again till he found a job, but his girl refused to see him. His old friends cut him dead in the street or crossed over to the other side when they saw him in the distance. The neighbors pulled the children inside and shut the door when he shouted "hello," and the shopkeepers asked him not to lean on their counters and did not want to sell anything to him, for they did not want to take money from his hands. And his own brothers and sisters refused to visit their mother while he was there.

His mother said, "Why not change your name and go away and begin life again in some faraway place?" But he said he would have to begin by lying about himself, and then he would have to keep on lying all along, and he said that would give him no peace of mind. So he decided to go back to the colony.

When my friend down at the stream told me this story about the young *sano*, the other women chimed in and said they had all experienced something the same.

Then someone said, "Do you remember that living skeleton of a woman who came a month ago? Well, another just as skinny arrived yesterday. They are both in the *vieja sala*, depressed and weak and hardly leave their beds, I'm told." A few months after this, I saw these two women in the queue for gifts. They did not look skinny any more. One was a *rubia* ("blonde") with blue eyes, and the other was a *morena* ("dark-haired"). I said to my washing companion, who had pointed this out to me, "How is it that they have lost their skinniness so soon?" "Food and freedom to mix freely with others act like a miracle," she said.

# Chapter 5: THE PROTESTANTS IN THE COLONY

## Apolinario and Marcelino

In the first years I was at the colony, Protestant pastors were allowed to visit and hand out gifts. They gave to everyone, no matter what his religion, but there were always grumblers, who were never content with what they got, and sometimes if they thought someone else had got something better, they called the pastors bad names.

Then suddenly the pastors stopped coming altogether. It was strange to see how the Protestant group melted away when the pastors were forbidden to come. Some kept away because they feared they would lose their jobs; others thought they would not get gifts at Christmas, and others thought they wouldn't be given a tender piece of meat in their provisions but only tough pieces.

So only a handful was left to meet on Sunday morning at Apolinario's. Apolinario kept a little shelf of books for those who could read. I remember one man became a believer before he could read, and then reading came very fast because he knew what the words meant in his heart, so he could figure them out in the print very easily. His name was Marcelino, and he lived with Apolinario and did all he could for him, both in the house and on the smallholding which they shared. But now Apolinario could not work in it anymore, as his hands and feet were so advanced in the disease. So Marcelino did all the work and also cooked for them both and dressed Apolinario's sores. They just kept enough of their produce for their own needs and gave the rest away to the poor. They also used to give me mandioca for my pig.

Marcelino had a daughter in Buenos Aires. She was so pleased to hear that Marcelino had got over his despair through his new faith. So she said she would like to help the people who had helped him to have trust in God. Marcelino asked her to help by sending them *Arco Iris* ("The

Rainbow") and *El Expositor Bautista* ("Baptist Expositor"). These were both Protestant papers. I liked them both, though *Arco Iris* was called a children's paper.

Apolinario had bundles of these papers on his little shelf, and he was glad to give them out to anyone who showed an interest. But often the interest was mainly in the paper on which it was printed. Paper was very scarce in the colony, and everyone had to bring paper wrappings for the things he bought at the little shops in the colony.

Then suddenly Marcelino died. Apolinario was very upset about it, and not only were all the Protestants very upset but also many of the poorer Catholics. Many of these spent money they could ill afford to buy big candles to light for Marcelino. There were people among them we hardly knew, but Marcelino had been kind to them. They all said, "Whatever his religion, he practiced charity." They also came to the funeral. Apolinario said a few simple words at the graveside, such as, "He that believeth in me shall never die," and everyone felt that just fitted Marcelino.

### In the *Calabozo*

The week after Marcelino's funeral, I had used up the last mandioca he had given me. Whenever I was running short of it, I used to go with my sack to Marcelino's plot of land, and he would dig some up for me. This time I took my spade with me, for Marcelino was no longer there to dig it for me. I had just started to dig, when a very angry man came running toward me shouting "*Ajeno* ['not yours']!" He would not listen to any explanations but said he was going off to get the police. In no time a police commissary arrived and marched me off to the *calabozo* ("jail"), but not before I had asked him to send word to my nearest neighbor.

It was Matilda-i. She brought me my poncho and some *galletas* and hot maté and said Mauricio had gone to tell Apolinario and that he would later see to my animals. Mauricio lived nearer me than Matilda-i and was always ready to help me, just like a son.

I was let out the next day. Apolinario was himself unable to walk far, but he asked a few who attended the Sunday *reunión* to go as fast as possible and explain to the commissary that I had been accustomed to come each week for mandioca and that I had no idea I was stealing.

When the commissary let me out, he said, "Doña Maria, I beg your pardon, but did you not know that a plot of land is snapped up at once, if no one is there any longer to cultivate it?"

**Prudencio**

After Marcelino's death, a young man called Prudencio moved in to look after Apolinario. As Apolinario's eyes were very bad, Prudencio read the Bible for him at the *reunión*, and Apolinario explained the meaning to those who could only speak Guaraní and didn't understand Spanish.

But Prudencio came from the town and knew nothing about land work, so he was unable to take over the smallholding Marcelino had worked. Prudencio worked in a metal workshop at the other side of the colony. So Apolinario was alone all day and sometimes confined to bed. But he was always cheerful, and if someone asked him if he was not lonely, he said, "It is always possible to enter into the presence of God, and no one can be lonely there."

Prudencio once said to me, "I will most likely never be able to get a wife in the colony, for all the girls are Catholics and don't like me because I am a Protestant." Prudencio was interested in the Bible and had faith to stand his ground, but it was not so with some others.

**Apolinario's Ways With People**

If a young man married a Catholic girl, Apolinario was still warmhearted toward him and toward the girl. This annoyed one or two very strict Protestants. Apolinario said, "Jesus never forced people; that is why He let himself be crucified. If those who want to force people into having faith would only remember that!"

Apolinario was also criticized because he would not disown Miguel, who sometimes drank too much and was put in the *calabozo*, for the doctor forbade strong drink to patients. Miguel's work mates used to say he was too thin-skinned for life, especially for the life of a *leproso*. He would drink when he got bad news from home, like hearing the older of his little girls, aged ten, had had to go out as a *criada* ("domestic servant") and then hearing that the younger one had to do the same. Everyone knew the dangers these children were running into, mostly from men but also from harsh mistresses, but Miguel felt everything more keenly than other people. Anyone who knew Miguel knew how he loved coming to the meetings at Apolinario's, and he loved the songs, and the singing was good when he was there, for he had a fine voice and kept to the tune. But after being let out of the *calabozo* he did not come to the meeting for a long time. He told Prudencio he would have come at once and never missed coming, but he knew the looks and the faces he would get from some. He and Prudencio worked in the same metal workshop, and he used to send home the money he earned, except when he lost heart and drank it away.

E.B.

Doña M.

## Our Christmas and Our Singing

At Christmas Apolinario used to play a few records on an old gramophone. Our favorite was "*Noche de Paz* ['Silent Night']." While it was playing, we would light the candles on the Christmas tree. The Christmas tree was a little bitter orange tree growing in Apolinario's patio, and we used to fix the candles into the firm green bitter oranges, and they made good candle holders. Many years later the same tree was still of use to us. It had long since grown too big to be our Christmas tree, but now it made a fine shade tree like an umbrella, and we used to sit under it at the meeting.

In our ordinary meetings we sang without the gramophone, and we listened to the meaning of the words and did not mind so much if the melody was not sung well. We felt strength and comfort in the words. There were songs for every mood—sadness, joy, or special occasions. We liked songs of comfort but also soldier songs with a marching tune, for a soldier must forget his own sorrows in the fight.

E.E

Doña M.

# Chapter 6: THE NEW REGIME—THE NUNS AND THE AMERICAN HOSPITAL

**The New Hospital**

Some years after I came to the colony, the old barn-like *salas* were replaced by a fine, new hospital building, with two parts—one the men's *pabellón* ("pavilion" or "ward") and the other the women's *pabellón*. The old *salas* were not pulled down till the hospital was complete.

We all watched with great interest. The tiled corridors and floors looked very fine, and we were glad we were to have such nice hospital buildings. We were told it was a gift from the North Americans, and later this fact was engraved on a big oblong stone, which was set into the wall of the main entrance. A lot of people didn't like that and said it was just politics. I thought it was very good of the North Americans to give such a gift, but then I have always been a *tonta* ("stupid woman") about politics.

Other people grumbled that some crucifixes, which had been there, had been taken down to make room for the hospital and had been thrown away. These people came to me and said, "That is what you Protestants do; you don't care for the Cross. You throw it out!" I said, "I think a good Christian carries the Cross in his heart, where you can't see it." And some folk said, "Yes, that is true."

**If You Will Bow Down and Worship Me**

The old *salas* were like big barns with thatched roof and wooden walls. Many poor folk were looking forward to their being pulled down, as they hoped to get some of the old timber. When they did get pulled down, folk ran there to get planks for their own use.

My young neighbor Mauricio was very poor. He had a kind of lean-to

66

shelter, and he was collecting wood to make a proper room for himself. He was there on the spot first thing in the morning, the day they began to take down the old halls, and he waited there the whole day. At nightfall, as he was passing my house, I thought he looked rather downcast. I shouted, "Hi, Mauricio, did you not have any luck?" He came over to me and showed me his empty hands. "I didn't even get a matchstick," he said.

"How is that?" I asked.

Then he told me there had been a big man standing there. He was a patient just like the rest of us, but he could talk about everything, and he was one of those who walk round with important visitors. If Mauricio tried to touch so much as one plank, he would shout "*ajeno* ['not yours']!" And if the big man left his post, he placed others there to shout.

Mauricio had been annoyed and went to see where the planks were being carried, and he found they were being used to make outhouses and pigsties for the rich patients, who already had nice dwelling houses of their own.

When Mauricio had told me all this, I felt sorry for the lad; he had worked so hard for the timber he already had. And I sat there at my doorstep sucking my bombilla, when Mauricio had gone, and thinking about it. Then I thought, "That is just the injustice in the world. The big man is like the devil, who possesses the world. He stands there, robbing the poor and giving it to his own."

## The New Regime

Four nuns were put in charge of the finished hospital buildings, and the old priest continued to visit the colony as before. Many changes were made in the colony after the coming of the nuns. There was no more serenading to be heard, and a new direction was given to couples living together. It was "marry or part." As time went on, there was less quarreling over women, and marriage became a regular practice, as it had not been before. But some people felt bitter about it.

Eugenio and Anastasia had to part. Anastasia went to live as a *camillera* ("ward maid") in the hospital, but she soon married. Eugenio lived alone. He carried on keeping his hens by good management, giving them food and water before going to work and closing them in after he got back. Mauricio also lost his *compañera*, because he said he would not be bossed in his private life or be ordered to marry; so the girl left him.

Another rule was made according to which any healthy wife who went about with other men was sent away.

There was a poor fellow Gregorio, very advanced in the disease, with a very pretty young wife. When she went out to get the stores, every second man played up to her. She found it too much of a temptation, so she gave in and was sent away. Poor Gregorio went a bit queer after that. People began to say, *"Falta tornillo* ['he has a screw loose'],” but I felt he just had a broken heart.

### Julio and Rosita

Then there was the romance of young Julio, the son of Felipa, with whom I once lived, when Julio and Braulia were children. Julio was now a young man in his late teens, and he made his living playing his harp at weddings, dances, or religious festivals, and sometimes he would play in the Roman Catholic church. He also played a lot at Alegria. This was an open-air amusement place, where there was a bandstand and folk could sit and listen to music or see a film or dance.

Rosita, a young girl in the charge of the nuns, fell in love with Julio. They got to know each other, as Julio used to smuggle notes into the dormitory where the girls slept. Some of the women told me that Rosita had been about six years old when she came to the colony. She came in a terrible state, for her family had just locked her in a room alone when they had heard she had leprosy, and Rosita was too small to understand why. It was pitiable to see her when she arrived—like a little frightened animal. Her people never had visited her since, so she came to look on the colony as her home and turned into one of the brightest girls there, with a voice like a bird and always singing.

So Julio and Rosita used to meet secretly, but one evening Rosita was not present at roll call in the dormitory. She got into trouble when she came in, and Julio was put in the *calabozo* for keeping such a young girl out so late. Rosita was very angry about Julio being locked up, so she ran away to Julio's mother, Felipa, and both of them went to visit Julio.

The *calabozo* is not like jails outside. You can have visitors; you can go for walks with them. The jailers are also patients. They will play cards with you or share a bombilla with you. The only thing is that you have to be locked in for the night. Julio had been put in there because Rosita was so young. However, when he was let out, they married, even though she was under age.

### Mauricio and the Worship of Images

Another thing that became a regular practice after the coming of the nuns was the carrying of images of saints on saints' days. These images were on stands, and the young men were expected to carry the stands. Then a tour was made of the colony, and the image was set down on the floor of a house, and the priest and nuns and others knelt and recited prayers. Then the stand and image were lifted and carried to the next house.

My young neighbor Mauricio used to say he was a "liberal" and did not believe in superstitions. On a saint's day he made sure he was not at home. He went out, anywhere—on the STICA land or on the campo, till it was all over.

Apolinario could not leave the house, even if he had wanted to, for his feet were so bad. Each saint's day he used to write something on his blackboard and put it at the entrance of his house. It was usually something like this, "God is a spirit and must be worshiped in spirit and in truth." Then Apolonario would just quietly sit in his hut, while the prayers were being recited, but everyone would know that was his answer.

I couldn't write, and I had no blackboard, but I just let them come in and recite their prayers and go. But I was sorry to hear on one saint's day that the nuns had asked Mauricio to help carry round the image. He had refused, because he said he did not believe in that kind of thing, and this offended the nuns, who knew he had been brought up in a Catholic orphanage and thus thought him ungrateful and a turncoat.

But Mauricio had a nature that couldn't be false. Other liberals could make a great show of pleasure when they saw the nuns and then mocked at them behind their backs. But Mauricio neither played up to them nor mocked them. He just was honest in what he believed, even though he knew he would be disliked. So he did not feel free to go and ask for all the bandages he needed for his bad feet. He used newspaper as a padding in his shoes, and he often came round to me to beg strips of old sheets or petticoats. I tore up all I had for him till I had nothing more. So he just sat down and took out his penknife and scooped all the mud from his sores, till the blood ran. I used to say, "Don't do that; you'll get tetanus."

"What else can I do?" he would say, and he went to work as usual the next day for STICA.

S.F.

# Chapter 7: OF LIFE AND PEOPLE IN THE NEW HOSPITAL

## Hospitalized Again

I took ill again and had to go to the hospital. I was terribly sick and had a splitting headache, so I could not get up out of bed. Neighbors told me I had been taking too much medicine and that too much always made folk feel like that and that I should leave off taking it for a bit.

This time the hospital where I was taken was the new North American hospital. What a contrast to the old barn-like building with its mud floor and windows with wooden shutters and no glass panes. This building had tiled floors and glass windows. It had a tiled corridor running down the center of the building and cubicles for two patients all the way along on either side of the corridor. The nuns ran it very well. Patients who were fit to work helped with the cleaning and cooking and nursing. The only folk in the two hospital *pabellones* who were not patients were the four nuns.

I did not see my cubicle companion for two or three days, for I had been too sick to notice anything. Then when I was able to take notice, I was a little put out to see a whole row of pictures of saints along her window sill. I wondered if she would be one of those people who would complain about my reading the Bible.

In the old barn-like *sala* you could push your bed far away from someone like that who was fanatical or from someone who was moody or who wanted to talk all night long or who didn't talk at all. Or sometimes there was someone who wanted her lamp on all night or the window shuttered up on a hot night or open in the cold weather. But I saw that here you had to stay where you were put.

Another thing I noticed when I felt a bit better was that the *camilleras* ("ward maids") were very bossy, and you could not make the place like home, because it had always to be quite tidy in case the doctor came to visit. And I was amazed to recognize the two big *camilleras* as the former living skeletons, who had arrived about a year ago. The blue-eyed one used to go up and down the corridor looking into the cubicles, and if she saw a patient's personal bits and pieces laid out on the small bedside cabinet, she would point to it and shout, "*Saca este cachivache* ['clear away that junk']!"

Some days later, when I was able to be up and out of bed, I used to go out on the veranda and talk with the patients who were sitting smoking or sucking their bombillas there. They all spoke praising the beautiful warm blankets on the beds, but none of them liked the tiled floors and corridors. One reason was that for those who could feel, they were cold to the feet, compared to the earthen floors which most patients had been used to. Another reason was that they were not allowed to bring their braziers into the cubicles or corridor. The only place they could have them was the veranda, which was open all along one side and often draughty.

The braziers were locked in a storeroom each night, and the dark-haired *camillera* had the key, but I never knew when to ask her to let me have my brazier. If I asked her when she was sitting down, she would say, "Don't you see I'm resting? Why didn't you ask me when I was on my feet?" And if I went to her when she was on her feet, she would say, "Don't you see I'm busy? Wait till I'm finished!"

### Perla and Galeano

In the cubicle opposite me across the corridor there was a very ill patient, a young girl, Perla. She could never get up out of bed, and she was getting weaker and weaker. She made the *enfermeras* ("patients acting as nursing helpers") angry. They said she made herself weaker because she wouldn't eat. She was such a beautiful young girl and barely out of her teens that I felt very sad over her. I went and spoke to her, and she said she just couldn't stomach the polenta or the *puchero*. "If only I had a nice, tasty little bit of *asado* the way we had at home, I'm sure I could eat that." So I went to Galeano, the hospital cook.

Galeano was a Protestant, and I had met him at the *reunión*. He did not mind who saw him read the Bible. He often had it in the kitchen with him and sometimes read it when he had a pause. He had to do the cooking for the men's and women's hospitals and for the big dormitories, and he had a lot to do, yet he was always ready to listen when anyone came and begged for some sick person. Other cooks never listened to special requests. They said, "Go and ask the nuns about it."

I had gone to the nuns and told them the young girl's wish, but they said, "If we ordered some *asado* for her, everyone would want the same, and we can't make exceptions."

Galeano was having a pause when I came to him and was reading the *Cruzado* ("The Crusader"), the Salvation Army paper, which he had in the kitchen with him. He listened to my request for a tender bit of grilling meat for the young girl. "What a shame," he said, "I could have given you a bit for you to grill for her, if you had come yesterday, but we have nothing suitable today." But when I came again another day, he did cut a nice, tender bit of meat, and I grilled it for her.

Perla was as pleased as a child. But she died soon after that, and I felt so sorry I had not done it for her more often. I noticed that some folk just got worse and worse and died as she did, and others got better and better and lost all signs of the disease. I could not understand, for both got the same remedies.

**Two Different Deaths**

There was a woman in the hospital called Limpia. She used to watch over the other women, and if any of them came near me when I was reading the Bible, she would whisper to them, "*Jaque, jaque!*" (Spanish for "check!" in the sense of "beware" or "watch out"). She was always quite pleasant to me apart from that. I could quite understand it, because Limpia was the strictest of all the Roman Catholics in doing all the things her religion asked for. She never missed going to mass, and she celebrated all the saints' days. She used to say the rosary very often, and she used to teach others to say it who did not know it. She also knew all the special prayers for special days, and every time the priest or nuns passed by, she used to ask them for a benediction. Most people respected her and obeyed her when she warned them against me. Of course, Eminencia did not heed Limpia's warning and came to me all the more, just to defy her, because she knew Limpia looked down on her in a self-righteous way.

But there was a nice, warmhearted little woman called Antonia. She was a Catholic but not fanatical or strict, and she used to face up to Limpia and say, "Why do you treat Doña Maria so? Aren't we all Christians, even if she is an Evangelical?"

Some time later, when I was well again and had returned to my *ranchito*, I went back to the hospital to borrow a big cooking pot, which was a gift for all the women to share. But no one would let me have it. One said, "It belongs to the hospital." Another said, "It is already promised for today," and so on. When Antonia heard them, she was angry and said, "You are just saying that because Doña Maria is an Evangelical. Take it, Doña Maria. It is quite clear it is for the use of all."

Soon after that, Antonia died. I was very sorry and went up to the hospital to ask about her. Everyone said how peacefully and happily she had died. She had said, "Don't mourn for me. I know it will be all right. Be happy and have a nice feast. I have put money aside for buying food. All who want to come are welcome—and don't forget to invite Doña Maria."

About the same time Limpia also died. She did not suffer much in body, but she was so afraid to die. For two days and two nights she cried out, "I'm going to die, I'm going to die!" The nuns tried to comfort her, but nothing helped.

I could not help thinking about these two women. The one had love in her heart for all—even for me, an Evangelical. The other obeyed all the rules and did everything she believed she should do. But God is only to be found in love, not in rules, and Jesus did not ask us to follow a single rule—only love.

## Deaths and Burials in the Colony

Deaths of the older patients usually took place in the cold weather, when many of them died of flu. When there was a death, the bell tolled in a special way, very slowly and dolefully. Friends would sit up with the body all night, with three lighted candles at the head and three at the feet, and none of them spoke.

The next day the funeral would take place, and after that folk would begin to chatter again. They would say, "Well, old so-and-so is in the *arroyo segundo* ['second stream'] now." We had a stream, which flowed through the colony, and that was where we did our washing. But the patients said we had another stream, and that was underground. This was in the cemetery, which was low-lying and so water-logged in wet weather, that the coffin made a loud splashing sound when it touched the ground at the bottom of the grave. Folk used to joke about the cemetery and say their only hope of leaving the colony was by way of the "second stream." But at the same time they hoped somehow that they would get out before it came to that.

### Eminencia

I wakened up the day after young Perla's funeral, because of such loud, angry voices coming from the veranda. I got up and went in that direction and asked a woman in a bed nearby what it was all about.

"Oh, it's that Eminencia; she is just shameless; she doesn't act as suits her age."

I asked her what Eminencia's age was. "I don't know—no one knows," said the woman.

I went out on the veranda and saw Eminencia. She was one alone against all the other women, who seemingly did not like her. Eminencia was now shouting at them. She called them "*caras duras* ['hard faces']" and "*víboras venenosas* ['venomous snakes']." And she shouted, "You don't have just one face—you have two or three faces!"

The women were furious, and one of them shouted, "You be quiet, you *tonta*! You don't even know how to say the rosary; you don't know the paternoster (Our Father) . . . you . . ." I felt sorry for Eminencia and said, "God loves a person, even if she can't say the rosary, and indeed it is written that He loves the *tonta* ['stupid one'] more than the *letrada* ['learned one']."

At that Eminencia was delighted and came and thanked me, and we became friends, and ever after she used to stick up for me if anyone was being unfriendly to me. If I wanted to take a lantern and go out and

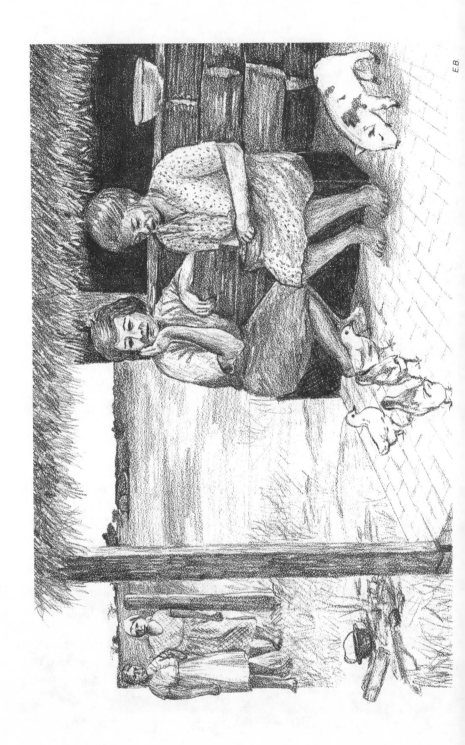

E.B.

another woman said, "No," she would rush in and say, "Who made you a boss here? Doña Maria has as much right to the lantern as you. It is for everyone."

Usually she got her own way, but if she were beaten in an argument, she would draw herself up in a very dignified way and say, "The one who holds her peace wins." She was a real character. She was a born play actress, and she had such a lot of different words in her head, and she could say the right ones for every occasion. And it was not just a few words; it was a flow of words coming fast, and she could act to fit the words. So wherever she was, you were sure to have a theater act.

The doctor used to notice her when he came on his visits and would say, "Ah! Eminencia is presenting herself," and they would have a laugh. But this used to annoy the other women, who said Eminencia was pushing herself forward. And they were even more against her when she tried her coquetry on the young men. She didn't like older men. But if a young man did not welcome her advances, she used to turn on him and call him a *"sucio leproso* ['dirty leper']," or she might sing something about him like this, *"Qué orgulloso, pero qué leproso* ['How proud yet how leprous']!"

Eminencia had a hatred for anything false or hypocritical, and her worst words came out for the folk who thought they were so good and sat in judgment on others. She also used to make up *burlas* ("lampoons") on these people and sing them aloud. These lampoons were very biting but often also very true. They were very much disliked, especially if they had some truth in them.

But Eminencia also had times of great depression. Then she would ask me to go with her to the crucifix in the forest, where she would kneel and weep for a long time, and I would stand a bit apart waiting for her and hoping she would find consolation.

I myself used to find great consolation in certain Protestant hymns, and Eminencia was the only Catholic who ever shared them with me. She would sometimes say, "Let us go off somewhere alone and sing that song of yours that I like," and we would go and sing:

*Though it is dark in the valley,*
*Yet it is light on the hilltop.*

### Of Cripples and Blind and the Nuns

Eminencia left the hospital shortly afterward, and I joined the group of women sitting on the veranda under a big notice, which said "Smoking prohibited," but no one took any notice of it. One little woman with no nose seemed to smoke small cigars all the time. She told me the smoke kept away the warble flies from what was left of her nose. She said the doctor knew we smoked and had remarked that anything acting as a pastime was good for patients who can't be active anymore.

The worst crippled woman was one whose legs were useless stumps, and she had to slide along the floor, lying on her stomach and using her elbows to move herself. She used to laugh and say, "*Aquí viene un perrito* ['Here comes a little dog']."

There was an old blind woman, who was so wise she knew the answers to almost any question you could put to her. She could remember dates too. Folk used to ask her, "How many years have I been here?" and she would say, for example, "Well, it will be twelve years this May." And she used to go through her laundry pile, feeling the clothes with her lips, as she had no sense of feeling in her hands, and she used to smell the clothes also. Then she would say, "This is not mine; I'm sure this is not mine," and sure enough there would be someone else's name on it.

Another blind woman had a son who used to send money to the nuns to keep for her. It was safer with them. Then the nuns gave her money for the things she wanted to buy, like sweets or cheese or cigars. Then she had to pay someone to go out and buy it from one of the little shops run by the patients.

There were quite a few women there with no fingers. One of them always kept bragging about her son. She said he was an aviator and also a first class soccer player. People in the end used to turn on her and say, "You would think you are the only person with a son," and then she would go away and cry. Once she said to me, "You have a son, Doña Maria, haven't you? Tell us about him."

"Yes," I said, "I have a son, and I hear he is a believer, and that makes me very glad."

"*Qué lindo* ['how nice']!" they would say and start talking about something else.

The women talked a lot about each other and about the doctor and about the nuns. Everyone had a great respect for the nuns, because we used to see them changing the dressings on the worst ulcers. We used to see the blood on their aprons and their hands. So we knew they were not afraid for themselves. But everyone's eyes were fixed on the nuns to see how they behaved to each other and to see if they had their little quarrels like everyone else. I watched them also, and I must say I only once noticed something between two of them. I could not hear what it was all about, but as they passed me, I heard one of them say to the other, "Well, I at least do not work to be seen of men!"

**Vicenta**

One day a new woman came to the *pabellón*. She was called Vicenta. What interested me was that she had a Bible and read it. She was quiet and sad and did not say much. I asked her if she was a Protestant, but she said no.

One day Vicenta had a visitor, who was a very beautiful and very *fifi* ("stylish, elegant") young girl. Everyone was most impressed, especially as the young girl put her arms round Vicenta and kissed her. It was Vicenta's daughter. Folk said she must love her mother very much to risk the contagion like that. We heard later that this daughter had given up her fiancé in Buenos Aires in order to come and be near her mother. She was earning good money in a small town nearby as a hairdresser, and she started straight away arranging to buy a nice, little house for her mother. So Vicenta did not stay long in the *pabellón*. I said to her, "Would you like to come and live with me till you have your own house?" She gladly accepted my offer. So when I was able to return to my own *ranchito*, I took her with me, and we lived together for a couple of months.

Each time before she took her medicine, she used to close her eyes and pray over it that it might heal her. Only then would she take it.

We used to discuss the Bible together, but the thing she was very keen on was to look up lots of passages to prove that Saturday was the proper Sabbath Day. She was the only person who celebrated it on Saturday, so she did not come to our meetings at Apolinario's.

I believe we should respect each other's faith, and I used to do so. But one day she asked me if I could get a letter writer to come and write a letter for her, as she had too shaky a hand to write anymore. I had difficulty in finding someone, and he said he would come after work on

Saturday afternoon. When I told Vicenta, she was quite worried and said, "Oh no! I could not pay a man to write a letter on the Sabbath Day."

### Of Women and Girls and the Nuns' Care of Them

Apart from the very incapacitated, most of the patients in the men's and women's wards of the hospital were only there because they had no little *ranchito* of their own. So patients used to work as far as they could and save the money to buy a little house or have one built.

But I noticed that few people were able to live alone unless they had some kind of faith. So there were always folk in both the men's and the women's wards who were looking for a partner with whom to set up house.

All the women were sought after, no matter what their age. While I was there, two seventy-year-old women married. One of them was a big loss to the women's *pabellón*, for she was a gifted storyteller, and both the young and the old enjoyed listening to her.

The nuns kept a strict watch over the women in the *pabellón* and used to put all the women's names on the roll call—not just the young girls. Each evening they used to come and sing a hymn in the *pabellón* and then call the roll and then say, "Good night."

The girls often used to sing with the nuns and then make a *burla* or skit on it, after the nuns had gone. One song was *"Quiero ir al cielo, al cielo, al cielo* ['I want to go to Heaven, to Heaven, to Heaven']," but the girls would sing, *"Quiero ir al suelo, al suelo, al suelo* ['I want to go to the ground,' or 'soil']."

The nuns were particularly strict with the younger girls, who were in their special care and who slept together in a girls' dormitory. The girls were not allowed friendships with boys or men. So any man or boy interested in a girl had to find indirect ways of letting her know. It had ended happily in the case of Julio and Rosita, which I mentioned earlier. But I was very sad about another marriage that happened while I was there.

There was a very nice, jolly tomboy of a girl called Chona. She was just full of fun and a friend of us all. She was simple and straightforward and had none of the tricks of the coquette. I used to notice one of the loud-voiced *gritones* ("bawlers") coming to the window of the cubicle where

old Olga slept. He would knock lightly and then push in a tray of grilled steak and tomato and some *dulce de fruta* ("fruit conserve"). I saw Olga get two or three nice meals like that. And then I noticed Olga calling Chona over to her and talking to her and giving her some titbits off the tray. In this way Olga acted as a go-between for the *gritón*, and the result was that Chona and he married.

I saw Chona shortly afterward and hardly knew her. She had become thin, and the smile had gone from her face. I said, "How are you getting on?" She just answered in a dull way, *"Regular* ['all right'].*"* She always said that, for she wanted to put a brave face on it, but I knew she was very unhappy.

There was a nice, quiet, elderly woman called Vera in the *pabellón*. We used to sit out on the veranda and share a bombilla of maté, and each day a man from the men's *pabellón* used to come and visit her. She did not encourage him at all and often used to go indoors when he came in sight, and one day she said to me, "Oh, here comes this man again— *parece permanentemente desocupado* ['he seems permanently unemployed']." Months later, after I had left the *pabellón*, I heard she had married him, and I was quite surprised.

## Chapter 8: MORE EXPERIENCES IN THE HOSPITAL AND BACK AT THE *RANCHITO*

### The *Turco*

I now felt so much better after my time in hospital that I took a daily walk to my *ranchito* to see how the animals were and how Pablo Berg was managing. He used to come each morning and evening and feed them and shut them up. He did this service for me free of charge because of his faith, which was his own and not any set religion.

Before going to visit my house I used to take a bucket of mandioca peelings with me from the hospital kitchen. Galeano the cook used to allow me to take what I could carry. But one day Abraham, a *turco* ("Turk" in the sense of "Armenian"), saw me set off with my bucket. He came after me and asked, "Whose bucket is that?"

I said, "It belongs to the kitchen."

Then he asked, "Where did you get the peelings?" and I said, "The kitchen."

"Then you don't have them," he said.

"But Galeano said I could," said I.

"*No importa* ['no matter']," said he and took the bucket away from me and dumped the peelings in the hospital pig bin.

I went to Galeano and told him. He said, "Abraham has no right to interfere. He is a patient like everyone else, and he has no post or duty connected with the kitchen or the pigs. He is just a born meddler. It is not the first time I have heard complaints about him. I think the poor chap must have been a big man outside, and now he has nothing and is nothing, and so he wants to show he was somebody important at one time by bossing and being officious."

When I told the women that evening in the *pabellón*, they said, "Oh, that *turco*! He does it to get in favor with the nuns, but if only the nuns knew that his religion lets him have lots of *compañeras* at one and the same time, while they make such a fuss over even one *compañera*!"

82

**By Pride Fell the Angels**

I had asked my neighbor Mauricio what would be a fair price for my calf that day when I went to visit my animals. He said, "Seven hundred guaranís." Mauricio was the young man who could not be false or hypocritical, and I trusted him completely.

I told the women in the *pabellón* that evening that I hoped to sell my calf for seven hundred guaranís. The news must have spread fast, for the very next morning Braulia came running to the hospital from her house at the far side of the colony. She came to ask if I would let her have the calf for one hundred guaranís down and the rest in slow stages later. I knew Braulia well, because I had lived with her and her brother Julio and their mother Felipa when they were children and when I had no *ranchito* of my own. Now Braulia was married and very badly off. Her husband was a guitarist, and he found it hard to earn a living, now that gramophones were taking the place of harps and guitars in the colony. I also had noticed that wives of musicians had all the heavy and rough outdoor work to do, for their husbands had to keep their hands soft and smooth. I felt sorry for Braulia and let her have the calf for one hundred guaranís down and the rest later.

The women in the *pabellón* had been listening to our conversation, and when Braulia had gone, they came up to me and said, "You've made a bad bargain there" or "You'll never see the rest of the money" or "Don't you know that pair are a couple of *verdaderos ladrones* ['real thieves']?" But they were wrong, for Braulia paid me the full sum in time.

These comments of the women in the *pabellón* did not upset me in the least, but I had two visitors at the time: Catalina, who had come with some copies of *Arco Iris* for me, and Eminencia, who asked if she could live with me for a bit. Catalina said, "You'd better let me keep the hundred guaranís for you, or you will give them away," and Eminencia added, "Or you will lose them."

I was quite offended and said, "No, I can keep them safely myself." So they went, and I tied the money in the corner of a white headkerchief that I had. Then I went home to get a second bed put up for Eminencia. The next day was Sunday, and Florenciana came to see if I was well enough to go to the meeting with her. She said, "Hurry, or we'll be late." It was a hot day, so I put on my kerchief to protect my head and neck. Florenciana walked so fast that I got too hot and pushed the kerchief back off my head and forgot about it. After the meeting, when it was time to go back to the *pabellón*, I noticed it was missing, with the money still tied in one corner! I looked everywhere in and around my *ranchito* and asked at all the houses on the way back to the hospital if anyone had seen it, and they all said no.

When I got back to the *pabellón*, already a few people were waiting for me. News had got around that I had some money, and one after another people came to borrow some.

I told them I had none. "But you got a hundred guaranís yesterday," they said. "Yes," I said, "but I've spent it." Then I realized I had lied. It had all happened so quickly, and I had not meant to lie. And I thought how cunning the devil was to make me do it, when I wanted to live telling the truth. Then I saw in a flash how he had managed it. He made me proud. I did not want the women to laugh at me and say, "There now, we told you so!" So I lied. And I remembered that the devil himself had fallen by pride, so he knows very well how to use pride to make others stumble and fall. I felt cast down about myself, but I knew I could forget myself and my failings by getting a fresh look at our Lord. This I found to be true, and I was also set free from my self-despondency, so as to think of others who might need a helping hand.

### So Be It According to Your Faith

At the Sunday meeting at Apolinario's we heard that Silvia had flu. Silvia had now and then come to these meetings, but then she stopped coming. She told us she still would have liked to come, but everyone had been at her—especially the nuns. They said it was sinful of her to come because she knew the true Catholic faith.

Now many people die each year of flu; they never die of leprosy. Leprosy weakens them, and then another illness, like flu, carries them off. So two of us from the *reunión* decided to go and visit Silvia that evening.

The other woman was Florenciana. She was a great one for herbal remedies and old country cures. When she heard Silvia had a painful chest, she set to at once to make her famous cough remedy. She had no difficulty in getting one of the young men to shoot an ani (a black cuckoo with a long tail) for her. She plucked it and made a rich bouillon out of it. It tastes the same as chicken, but it is cheaper, as anis are so plentiful. Then she put some carpincho oil into the soup.

We met at Florenciana's *ranchito* and waited till the remedy was ready. When we got to Silvia's house, one of her neighbors, Dorotea, was already there. She had brought a little bottle with tablets of aspirin and was telling Silvia what a wonderful remedy it was for nearly everything— colds, headaches, and aches and pains of all sorts.

Then Florenciana put her ani-and-carpincho-oil soup on the fire to warm, and Silvia said, "Oh, how good of you! That was the remedy my grandmother always used for chests. It is good, and my chest hurts. I'll take some as soon as it is warmed up."

Dorotea gave Silvia the aspirin and told what a good cure it was for everything. But just then Dolores, another woman who attended the *reunión*, came in. She was a believer in faith healing and said it was not faith to take remedies. She said, "Don't take the tablets or the soup—just have faith and leave the remedies!"

"But," said Silvia, "my old grandmother used to cure us all of chest trouble with the same remedy as Florenciana's. It is the best remedy for coughs and chest pain."

"Have faith!" said the faith-healer woman.

"But my chest hurts," moaned Silvia.

Then I felt I must chime in, for it was cruel to Silvia. So I said, "You can't order a person what to believe, Dolores. You yourself believe in faith healing; so that is the best remedy for you, and if another person has some belief in it, you can encourage it, but you can't make it. Dorotea believes in aspirin, and Silvia and Florenciana believe in carpincho oil in soup. The best thing to help a person is to give them what they have faith in. Jesus even said, 'So be it done unto you according to your faith.'"

They all agreed that probably that was so, and Silvia sighed with relief, as she sipped her hot soup and carpincho oil.

### Back to the *Ranchito*, With Eminencia

The next day I took leave of the nuns and thanked them for their care. One of them said, "You are German, Doña Maria, so I suppose you belong to the Lutheran Church?" I said, "I have never heard of that kind of Church. I don't rightly know what kind of Church I belong to. I just believe in Christ."

"Oh," she laughed, "you just hug the Bible—that is your religion."

When I got home, I found Eminencia was already there. She said her *compañero* had been beating her, so she had run away. So I let her stay as long as she wanted.

She used to want to come with me to the *arroyo* and help me with the washing that I took in, but if I let her help me, I always heard about it afterward, when I gave the washing back. My customers would say, "Good day, Doña Maria, have your hands got bad?" or "Is your strength going, Doña Maria?" "No," I would say, "why do you ask?" "Well, Doña Maria, your washing is not the same as it used to be."

Also, the folk who thought well of themselves used to keep asking me, "Do you not know what kind of woman you have under your roof?" Eminencia was with me for barely a week, for she soon found another *compañero* and left me. But she always remained friendly to me, and ever since, whenever she met me, she would put her arms around me and say, "Ah, Doña Maria, *mi única amiga* ['my only friend']!"

The day after she went was a Sunday, and I was surprised to see Vicenta at the *reunión*. She was the woman with the *fifí* ("elegant") daughter whom I had met in the *pabellón* and who thought that the Sabbath should be celebrated on Saturday. Apolinario listened to her with respect for her beliefs, the way he did to all folk who had other faiths.

**On Pigs**

Vicenta was now living in the house her daughter had bought her, and she told us her daughter had also paid for a nice, big fence of slats of wood put close together round her house. That was a fine gift, for then she could grow vegetables without people's animals coming and eating them or scratching them up. I was very interested in the fence, just as we all were, for we all would have liked one. Vicenta asked me to come and visit her, which I did. The fence made a fine, big enclosure, and she had a little bit of garden by the door and a wire enclosure for some hens in one corner. I said to Vicenta, "Why, Vicenta, you have plenty of room also to fence in a pig in that far corner."

Vicenta was a bit startled. "Pig, did you say?" she said. "I would never have a pig; they have the devil in them."

"However do you make that out?" said I. "I've heard them called dirty, but I have never heard that."

*Doña M.*

"Have you never read how the devils in the madman asked to be allowed to enter the pigs?" said she.

"Yes," I said, "but that was long ago, and those pigs are all dead now."

"No," said Vicenta. "That meant the devils were allowed to enter the whole race of pigs—not just those."

"Well, it didn't say so," said I. "It spoke only of a herd of pigs and said they tore down the hill and got drowned in the lake. You could say those pigs did a good service getting rid of those devils."

"You can't drown a devil—he is a spirit!" said Vicenta.

"Oh, I suppose you can't," said I, "but I have seen much more of the devil in men than in any pig I have reared, and I know pigs well. I always bring the young ones into my house in the cold weather, and I have never lost one. There is no kindlier mother animal than a sow."

"Whatever makes you say that?" said Vicenta, who was a town dweller.

"Well, I have reared many litters of piglets, and I have watched how gentle the sow is. She will try and lie down half a dozen times and get up at once if one of the young piglets squeals, for she does not want to lie on it and hurt it. Now a hen is the very opposite. She won't take any notice if she has put her foot on a chick, no matter how loudly it peeps."

"But they are such dirty animals," said Vicenta.

"No," said I, "they are cleaner than most other animals. They like to keep their bed straw clean and do so if given a chance."

"I don't know anything about that," said Vicenta. "All I know is that I was brought up to believe the pig was the incarnation of the devil, as they call it, and I was taught to avoid the pig, whether living or dead."

"How can that be?" said I, "when the pig is also called the poor man's friend?"

Vicenta didn't answer, so I continued, "There is no animal so profitable as the pig. And there is no fat to equal pig fat. It never tastes old like cooking oil, and it never sticks to your mouth when it is cold the way cow fat does."

"We will not quarrel about it," said Vicenta. "That is just the way I was brought up."

So we began to talk about something quite different, and neither of us ever mentioned the subject of pigs again.


**Filthy Rags**

Vicenta used to like to wear white. She said it was a sign that she was saved.

I never liked the idea of "holy" clothes of any kind. I always felt it was a kind of pride and parade. I asked Apolinario what he thought about it, and he said, "Man's goodness is never more than filthy rags before God," and he added, "Jesus even refused to be called 'Good Master' and said, 'No one is good—only God.'" Then Apolinario told me a little story.

Once there was an artist in Buenos Aires. One day he ran into a beggar in the streets and thought, "That is just the model I need for my picture." He gave the man his address and some money and asked him to come next day. The beggar was delighted and spent the money on a bath and shave and haircut. Then he got a nice suit in a second-hand shop and a pair of shoes. When he turned up at the artist's house, the artist did not recognize him. The beggar said, "You asked me to come, so I've come."

"Oh," said the artist, "you should have come as you were. Now that you've cleaned yourself up, I can do nothing with you."


**God Can Soften Men's Hearts**

One day my cat caught a lizard and started playing with it. Lizards are innocent creatures, which do no harm but just eat flies and other insects.

I tried to rescue the lizard, but the cat just growled and bit harder. The lizard made no sound. He just looked at me with his big eyes. I did not like to see it being tortured, and I thought God must surely have pity for it. Just as I was thinking this, the cat saw something in the distance that interested him—perhaps another cat. Anyway, the cat let go of the lizard, and it was able to run off. I wondered if God had softened the cat's heart, the way He does with people we pray for. Vicenta once told me that had happened with someone she had prayed about.

Vicenta had very trembling hands and could not get through her household jobs in time to suit the butcher. The butcher liked to divide up the meat early and then shut up shop. If people did not come in time, he would send the rest of the meat to the hospital, and late-comers were told to go there.

The nun in charge used to say, "All the meat is in the big pot; you should get to the butcher earlier. I can't do anything about it now." This had happened quite often to Vicenta. Then Vicenta prayed that God might soften the nun's heart. And the next time she was late, the nun said, "Here, I've kept a bit of meat for you, Doña Vicenta. You can't be losing your meat ration each week."

Doña M.

# Chapter 9: ABOUT MARTÍNEZ, GALEANO, AND PABLO BERG

## No Wind in the Corral

Now that I was back at my little house again, I started catching up on the jobs I had neglected about the house, while I was sick in the *pabellón*. I started collecting wood again for my fire, and I went with a sack to Martínez, the carpenter, for wood shavings for kindling.

Martínez used to say he was an *agnóstico* ("agnostic"), yet I thought he saw the truth of many things more clearly than some of the very religious people. Anyway, I always remembered the things he said, and I thought about them, and I believe Jesus would agree with a lot of it.

One day when I went to him after my work, the vespers bell was ringing in the little church. This annoyed him. He said, "Just listen to those bells. That's to tell you to pray—but you can't just turn on the tap like that. That's the trouble with so many religious folk. They want to regulate everything by bells or rules and orders. But that is not true religion. True religion is free—as in Pablo Berg, the 'prophet.' His religion is an adventure! He obeys no boss except something inside him, which bears him up above his poverty and advanced disease and takes away all fear of men, so that he tells them what he thinks of them when they bully the weak. His religion is like the rushing of the wind, which blows where it wishes and won't be shut in. But those whose religion fences them in by outward rules find no wind comes into the corral (cattle enclosure)."

## The Dotted Line

One day when I went to get shavings in the carpenter's shop, there were three old men there before me, all asking for shavings. One of them

90

was wearing a beautiful, brand-new poncho. He was telling the others how they could get one too. He said, "The priest has a big pile of them. All you have to do is to attend mass and be pleasant and polite to him."

Martínez heard this and said, "You're asking them to sign on the dotted line."

"What do you mean?" they asked.

"Well," said Martínez, "you know what I mean: Attend mass, be respectful, agree with everything, and all will be well—plus ponchos!"

One of the old men replied hotly, "I am not going to sell my soul for a poncho!"

Then Martínez turned to me and said, "You read the Bible, don't you, Doña Maria, and know about Peter and the pearly gates?"

The old men nodded, but I was not sure where Peter came into it—I only was certain about Jesus Christ. Martínez then gave a sweep of his hand and said, "Well, anyway, I'm sure when Peter, or whoever it is, goes through your records at the pearly gates, he will frown at all the dotted lines you have signed on, especially if they are religious ones. And then he will say, 'How much did you let the wind of the Spirit blow through you?'"

**About Burials**

Yet another thing I remember about Martínez was a conversation about burial. He was laughing at those who believed an unchristened infant would go to Hell and should not be buried in the "holy" ground of a churchyard. Then he added, "But I don't believe in burial anyway, especially of *leprosos*. I think *leprosos* should be cremated. It would protect other people by getting rid of the leprosy bacilli."

But the Roman Catholics present would not hear of cremation, because the Pope was against it, and that was the final word for them. Some Protestants standing by agreed with the Catholics in this. Then Martínez turned to me and said, "What do you think about it, Doña Maria?"

I had been thinking to myself about it, and I told them what my thoughts were. I said, "I don't think it matters at all."

"Why do you say that?" they asked.

"Well," I said, "many saintly men got burnt alive, just because they followed Jesus more than other men did."

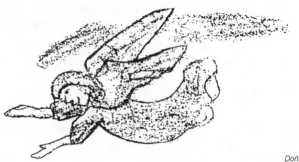

**Pablo Berg**                                                          *Doña M.*

Martínez never came to our *reunión* at Apolinario's, but occasionally
Pablo Berg came. I remember the first time I met Pablo was at
Apolinario's, years ago, when I first started taking in washing. Ever
since, I had washed for Pablo free of charge, for I was so struck by his
kind of loyalty to Christ. He told us he had once had a vision of Christ and
a red devil. This vision had changed his whole life, and he remembered
it so well that he could never like the color red ever after. Once a batch
of pink shirts were being given out as gifts, and he refused his, because
he said pink was just a faded red! I knew how ragged his other shirts
were, but he would not yield.

He said the devil had offered him a career and riches if he refused
Christ, and Christ had said, "If you follow me, you will never refuse a
service to the poor, but the angels will accompany you." Pablo chose the
latter, and that meant he was the poorest person in the colony. He lived
in the men's *pabellón* (dormitory), and his only possessions were a water
jug, a bombilla, and the stick he leaned on to walk.

He also was poor because he was so outspoken that he offended people
who could have given him clothes. He told me he once went into the
Roman Catholic church just to see what it was like. He saw men go in
with their machetes (bush knives) in their belts, and he thought, "That is
not right to go into a place of worship taking your carnal weapons with
you." Then he watched the people at prayer, and one lifted his poncho
and got his money out and started counting it, and another got his machete
out and started feeling the blade. So when the service was over, he went
to the priest and said, "I've been watching your flock at prayer, and I
would say your flock are goats—not sheep."

"You must have patience with them," said the kindly old priest.

## Galeano's Death

Pablo used to collect his clean washing from me and sometimes he would sit and rest his feet before going back to the men's dormitory. Galeano the cook also slept there. He had begun to find the kitchen work too much for him; he got so tired and was doing less and less. When he came to the *reunión*, we noticed he was getting more and more yellow. The doctor said he must not eat salt, but that was difficult, because the meat and polenta (corn mush) were all salty.

One day he could not get up anymore. Pablo Berg slept in the same dormitory and told me about him. He said Galeano would just lie in bed and read the Bible. This annoyed Rita, a patient working as an *enfermera* ("nurse helper") and a fanatical Roman Catholic. Rita was always making digs at him about his faith. One day she said, "This is the fiesta of San Juan (St. John's Day), but he doesn't mean anything to you, does he?"

"Indeed, Rita, you are wrong," said Galeano. "The wooden San Juan that you carry around means nothing to me, but the real San Juan means a lot. That is why I read the Gospel he wrote." When Galeano had said that, he lay back, and you could see he was ill. The Sister Superior, who had heard the conversation, noticed it and said, "Now, now, Rita, we are not here to argue about religion but to serve the sick."

The priest, Padre Ochoa, was a fair-minded, humble, and kindly man, but he had some fixed ideas. He felt sorry to see Galeano approach death without confession and absolution and believed it was his duty to try and get him to confess and receive absolution before he died. But Galeano always refused. He said, "There is no need for anyone but Christ to forgive my sins; that is why He died. I believe in Him, and I need no one else. Thank you for wanting to help me, but I wish you had what I have in this hour through faith in Christ—the Savior and my Savior."

He died soon after that. Pablo told me the man in the next bed had said, "I admire a good Protestant." "So do I, so do I," added other voices round the dormitory.

*Doña M.*

## More About Pablo Berg

I would always go to Pablo when I was in trouble. Once our bell-ringer came to me very hot and angry. He said I owed him a big sum, because my cow had eaten two sacks of his corn and that if I did not pay, he would have my cow taken from me. I went and told Pablo, and he put it all right for me. He went to the bell-ringer and asked how many times the cow had come. "Once," said the bell-ringer. Then Pablo proved that no cow could eat two sacks of corn at one go. So the bell-ringer dropped the matter.

On rare occasions Pablo would come to the *reunión* at Apolinario's. He told us his father had been a Jew and his mother was a native of the land here and a Roman Catholic. Pablo liked to talk to us about his ideas and about the Book of Revelation. Apolinario always welcomed him and listened to him; he would say, "No one has the whole truth; the truth is *inmensa* ['immense']." Pablo would have long talks with Apolinario and used to say that he was a Jew with a Christian reverence for Christ. Apolinario would say afterwards that Pablo had more real reverence for Christ than many Christians.

Other times when Pablo came to the *reunión*, he would stay on afterward and talk about things that had happened to him at the men's dormitory.

He told us that on fiesta days (saints' days) there were long "vain repetitions" recited in the dormitory, and later *caña* (rum from sugar cane) would be given out.

He said, "I just take my stick and go out into the corridor till it is all over, for I am neither for the one nor for the other."

He also told us that once he could not escape so easily. He was in bed in the morning, but he was still asleep. Then he was wakened by chanting. When he opened his eyes, he saw that there was a circle of people holding lighted candles and chanting round his bed. It was the priest, the nuns, and some other people. Pablo said he sat up in bed and said, "I'm not dead yet, and I'm not a Catholic." They continued chanting as if nothing had happened, and he kept sitting up and waving his hands to say, "Pipe down!" Then a nun quietly tiptoed over to him and whispered in his ear that it was not for him they were doing it but for someone who had died in that bed, and this was the anniversary.

Pablo then told of another thing that had happened in the *pabellón*. One of the oldest patients there had not been well for some time. He was one of the very first patients to be sent to the colony, when it was not much more than a distant ranch, which served as an isolation place. The dilapidated old ranch buildings made a shelter for the patients, but they had no food rations from the government at that time.

The old man took a bad turn and began to sink fast. He wanted to confess something, but the priest was away, and the nuns all busy elsewhere, and the old man was begging to get something off his chest. So Pablo had said to him, "I myself believe only in confessing to God, but if it will ease you, you can confess to me, brother." Then the old man said that in those days when they had to find their own food and were tired of wild bitter oranges and other wild forest foods, he had killed an ox belonging to a neighboring *estanciero* ("rancher"), and they had some grand meals.

"Is that all?" said Pablo. "You did well to feed the hungry." With that the old man closed his eyes and died.

Pablo was really a very ill man, but he always said he was all right, and he never concerned himself about his health. He had leprosy, both of his face and of his hands and feet, and he had a war wound, which had never healed. But his spirits carried him much further than many a healthy man will go. Sometimes he would leave the colony and go off to warn people of the end of the world and that they should repent. On these trips he used to sleep in the forest and eat what he could find there.

Once a group of men with angry faces and machetes drawn came toward him and shouted "*Leproso!*" Everyone could see it from his face and hands. The men said he was spreading the contagion and that they would put a stop to that.

Pablo said, "Are you Christians?"

"Yes."

"Do you believe what the Bible says?"

"Yes."

"It says, 'Thou shalt not kill.'"

Then they put away their machetes. "It is because the angels were with me that they could not harm me," he said afterward.

Just after Easter each year a straw man was made and filled with fireworks and set on fire, and people used to say it was Judas Iscariot. Folk used to say to Pablo, "Jews, like you, crucified Christ!"

Pablo would say, "Show me a picture of the crucifixion and the sepulcher. See, there are Roman soldiers in both. The Romans had a big hand in it, and why then are you so proud to be called 'Roman Catholics'? And anyway, you don't seem to know the Bible: Judas was never burnt; he hanged himself."

But Pablo's stomach began to bother him a lot, though he said nothing but just got even thinner. He could not keep down the food that was cooked in the one big pot. So at the latter end of his life I offered to cook for him, and this he was able to eat better. He used to come to my *ranchito* and eat it.

Pablo had to sit and rest a bit before walking back to the *pabellón*, for he had lost strength since becoming so much thinner. While he was sitting, I would ask him about his earlier life.

## Pablo Berg's Earlier Life

He told me he had married when he was still in his teens and knew nothing about life. His wife was older and knew a lot. The marriage was not happy. She spent money right and left without limit, and he would often say, "Do you think you have married a gold mine?" The loss of his money did not worry him so much, but it was quite a different matter when he found out she had a lover. He told her he was not going to play second fiddle and that she could go to the other man, and he left everything and joined up as a soldier in the Bolivia-Paraguay war. He was in it right from the beginning to its end.

It was terrible, the hardships they went through: hunger, wounds, thirst—terrible thirst, and insects of all kinds eating them alive. He said he dated his leprosy from then.

He said he did not believe in killing, so he used to fire his rifle to one side or into the air to avoid killing anyone. Then he went home on leave—not to his wife but to his mother and sister. His father was long since dead. When he told them all he had been through in the war, they begged him to wear an amulet, for they were strong Roman Catholics.

He took it unwillingly, for he had always leaned more to his father's faith. Then, as soon as he was back in the fighting, he got wounded in the hip. He said he felt it was his punishment for taking part in idolatry. The wound never properly healed and lasted as a running sore till his death.

He used to tell the men at the *pabellón* about the amulet and showed them his wound. This did not please the people who were giving out amulets to comfort the patients, so he was not liked by them and missed getting the help they could have given him in other ways.

### A Cool Place for an Opossum

One day I had given Pablo a maté bombilla after his meal, and he was sitting sucking it and saying nothing. Suddenly he pointed to my *cántaro* ("water pitcher") and said, "Look!"

I kept the *cántaro* on a tall stand out of the reach of any animal that might have wanted to drink out of it. I looked and was amazed to see a wet-haired little head peep over the rim of the *cántaro*. The head began to turn in all directions and gaze around with big, blinking eyes, which were dazzled by the sunlight. It was a *comadreja* ("opossum"), and they can't see in the daytime. It must have gone into my drinking water to cool itself, for it was the hottest part of the year. Then it climbed out, all dripping wet, and ran away, with its long hairless tail trailing behind it.

Pablo said, "I thought your maté tasted a bit strange, but I thought you had put one of your *yuyo* ['herbal'] remedies in it."

## Pablo's Death

One day not long after that, Pablo told me his hands were making it difficult for him to fasten on his shoes. As he had no toes, he had to fasten the shoes on well, or they came off. And to make it even more difficult, his shoes were split, and he held them together by binding wire round them. But he laughed and said he often thought of the elastic-sided house slippers he had had at home when he was young and had no need for then, and now how useful they would be, and no trouble to his hands to fasten them. It was not only his hands that were getting worse, but his legs were less able to walk.

One evening, after he had eaten, I noticed he could hardly stand when he got up to go. He said, "It will pass" and sat down again. Each time he got up it was the same, and night was coming on. So I fixed up my canvas bed, which I used in the very hot weather, for him. It folded into a chair at other times, and Pablo was so light he would not break it. So he slept there all night and went back to the *pabellón* next day.

I did not see him for some time after that, and then when he next came, he told me the nuns had made such a to-do because he had slept under my roof. They said it was wrong and shameless. Pablo was angry and said, "Why don't you send a spy to see what I am doing? I have a wife of my own outside and do not break my marriage vows to her. If I did, the angels would leave me."

After I left for Primavera, he died in the *pabellón*. I was very cut up about it, when I heard of it. He had been a true friend to me, and though I did not agree with all his ideas, yet God will accept him, because he never refused to do a service to a poor person who asked him.

M.

# Chapter 10: LIFE AS AN INVALID, ALSO ABOUT CATALINA AND MATILDA-I

## A Crippling Fall

For years now I had been doing some washing of other people's clothes, to make a little ready money. When I was saving up to buy my animals, I did a lot of washing; now I did much less but sold young animals instead, when I wanted money.

Washing was not easy work, for the *arroyo* was down a steep incline, and the basket of wet clothes was very heavy to carry home up the hill.

One day I was trying to steady a basket of wet clothes on my head, and my feet were not too good that day, so I stumbled over a rock and gave myself a big shake-up. I had to rinse all the clothes again down in the stream.

The next morning I could not get up out of bed. I had such a pain. I called Matilda-i ("little Matilda"), my neighbor, to come and make a fire, as it was such a cold morning. But Matilda-i was a great worker. She never missed the clock-in at STICA, where she worked, and she was proud of her record. Though she heard me call to her, she shouted, "The work bell has gone; I must be off, or I'll be late."

So I had to lie in bed all day, cold and hungry. When evening came, I listened for the first neighbor returning home. It was Mauricio. I called him and asked him to fetch a woman neighbor. He did so, and she sent a message for a stretcher to take me to the hospital.

## Publicans and Sinners

Poor Matilda-i was very upset when she came home and found me being lifted on to a stretcher by two *enfermeros*. And the neighbors had one or two sharp words for her too. She had not meant it badly, but she

100

was just one of those folk whose be all and end all is work. She was a *sana* and had supported herself and a severely ill, bed-ridden husband for years. He could not earn at all. He had a very weak stomach and couldn't eat mandioca, which was our main food, so she had to buy many extras for him.

She was always friendly and helpful to me, but I often heard men say, "She is worth nothing," or, "She is everyone's woman," and they used to look down on her. I would feel sorry for her, for I used to think she is bound to feel it when they call her *perra* ("bitch"), and she can't have a high opinion of herself.

And then I thought, "But these are the folk there is most hope for, because they are the folk Jesus came for—not the self-righteous!" That is how it was when Jesus was on earth: The first person He spoke to after He arose had been a prostitute (till she met Him). And the first person He welcomed into Paradise with Him was a condemned thief, who believed.

### Trusting That God Is Powerful

I got much better after lying up at the hospital, but the doctor said I would not be able to do any more washing down at the stream. And he also said I would not be right again until I had had a big internal operation. I asked him if he could do it, and he said, "Oh, no, I'm not a surgeon." No one had ever heard of a surgeon coming to the colony, especially for a poor person. I was also told that surgeons charge a lot of money. I did not know what to do, but I got a friend to write a letter to my husband about my fall and the operation that I needed done. I knew he had no money any more than I had, but I just trusted something would happen. I thought, "God can work in ways we don't know anything about." I waited and waited and heard nothing, so I stopped thinking about it and turned my attention to the day-to-day happenings in the women's *pabellón*.

There was great excitement, for we heard that the seventy-year-old storyteller was coming back to the *pabellón*, as her marriage had broken up. I was able to hear one or two of her stories, before I returned to my *ranchito*. I found some days I could do my work, but other days I had to neglect everything, and my animals wandered far in search of food.

Vicenta and other friends used to come and visit me, if I had not

managed to go to the meeting on Sunday morning. They would say, "You
can't go on like this! Aren't you doing something more about it?"
"What can I do?" I would say. "I am a *tonta*, and I have no money.
God will find a way, for God is powerful."

So I thought no more about it and just waited and went on with my
work as best I could, and some days it was a very poor best. When I did
not feel able to work, I just sat outside my door, sucking my bombilla.

**Gregorio**

One day I was doing that, and my black cat Puracola ("nothing but
tail") was sitting on my lap, when I saw Gregorio coming down the path.
He was the man whose pretty wife was sent away from the colony. Now
the poor fellow was like a scarecrow. His feet were so bad that he had to
walk with his arms out like a bird flying, so as to steady himself. He was
shouting "*Satanás* ['Satan']!" Mauricio was coming down the path in
front of him, so I shouted to Mauricio, "What have you done to Gregorio
to make him call you '*Satanás*'"?

"He's not calling me *Satanás*," said Mauricio. "He is calling it to José
and Marina Valenzuela."

"Why should he be doing that?" I asked.

"Don't you hear the noise? They are celebrating a birthday at their
house, and Gregorio is angry he hasn't been invited."

I listened, and sure enough I heard singing coming from Marina's
house and loud laughter. Then a man with a pistol came out of her door
and fired it into the air again and again and shouted, "*Viva Paco* ['long
live Paco']!" and the others shouted "*Viva Paco!*" It was Paco's birthday.

Paco and other single men used to eat at José and Marina Valenzuela's
house. They brought their rations and paid Marina to cook for them.

There were often birthday celebrations there, and sometimes Marina brought me some titbit from them.

### In Christ There Is Neither Male nor Female

This happened some weeks later, when Catalina was visiting me. Catalina was a Protestant; she had had a good education and was one of those who could read and write well. She also had faith, so I used to listen to things she said in talks with other people, for they were often worth remembering. Now she had come to bring me *Arco Iris*, which I liked. It was simple but very true and easy to read.

When Marina saw Catalina, she said, "I should give this *dulce de fruta* ['fruit conserve'] to you, not Doña Maria, for it's your birthday today."

"No," laughed Catalina, "it's not my birthday!"

"But it must be surely," said Marina, "for today is *Santa Catalina's* ['St. Catherine's'] Day."

"I was not called after *Santa Catalina*," said Catalina, "but after Catalina Booth."

"Oh, but that's an upstart religion," said Marina. "It's barely one hundred years old. Ours goes back to the day *San Pedro* ['St. Peter'] was given the keys."

"True religion is always new," said Catalina. "It happens when Christ lives in the heart of the believer and gives him forgiveness and new life."

"Maybe so," said Marina, "but Catalina Booth was wrong. She used to preach and allowed other women to preach, so she disobeyed *San Pablo* ['St. Paul'], who forbade women to preach."

"Yes, that was often said to Catalina Booth," said Catalina. "But Catalina Booth said there is nothing in the Gospels that forbids it, and when the Spirit was poured out at Pentecost, it was poured on both men and women. *San Pedro* was present when this happened, and he said the old prophet Joel had said this would happen, and then the sons and the daughters of men would prophesy."

"You are forgetting *San Pablo* forbade women to speak in public," said the other woman angrily.

"When that was said to Catalina Booth," said Catalina, "she used to say, 'If God calls a woman to preach and she obeys instead the prohibitions of men and refuses to say what the Spirit of God wants her to say, she runs the danger of quenching the Spirit.'"

"But that is making women equal to men!" said Marina. "I am surprised at you, an Evangelical, not knowing your Bible better. Don't you know that Eve was made from one of Adam's ribs? Now that surely means they are not equal. Isn't that so?"

"In physical strength they are not equal," agreed Catalina, "and often not in brains, but in Christ they are equal. The Bible says, 'In Christ there is neither male nor female.'"

When both Catalina and Marina had gone, I continued sitting and thinking. And I thought, "If only people would not argue about each other's faith!" And I thought, "Surely God uses all kinds of instruments for His harvest. He does not work only with a machete. He also needs spades and hoes and *cuchillas finas* ['fine knives for pruning']."

**Matilda-i**

Someone who often came to visit me after my fall was Matilda-i. I think she was glad that I did not blame her the way other neighbors did for not coming to my help, when I called to her that morning after my fall. We just used to pass the time of day before, but now I got to know all about her, as she came so often and liked to sit and talk and tell me her story.

She told me her mother had been one of the first women patients to be sent to the colony in the very early days, when the place was little more than a run-down ranch. Times were very hard then. There was no medical care and no governmental food ration. They used to collect wild food— even the bitter oranges in the forest.

Matilda-i and her sister, Piadosa, and two brothers had been born in the colony in the early days, when there was no preventorium (a home where children liable to develop the disease receive preventive care) in the big capital, where children of patients were sent in later years. Any child born in the colony in those days just lived with his mother and risked leprosy rather than starving outside. None of those four children knew who their fathers were, except that they were patients.

The mother died when they were in their teens. The children remembered little of the hardships their mother had to bear, for they hardly remembered a time when there were no government food rations.

All grew up fit and healthy, and as they were now young adults, with no infirm mother to look after, they were all sent out of the colony.

The two boys soon found work as cattle men for nearby *estancieros*. The girls became *compañeras* to men who had small *chacras*. Their main diet was mandioca (the staple starch food of South America) and maize, as with the local poor. They also had a little meat, supplemented by what their *compañeros* could trap or snare. This might be an armadillo or a land crocodile or, if they were lucky, a carpincho, or even now and then a monkey, which had come to steal the maize. The *compañeros* thought both girls were *mimadas* ("pampered, spoilt") and *delicadas* ("fussy"), for they could not bear to skin and cook the monkeys, which they said were too much like humans.

So both girls came back to the colony and became wives or *compañeras* to patients. They said they now understood why the people outside steal so much. They said you could no more blame them than a hungry dog. Matilda-i was happily married to a patient. The only thing that bothered her was the banning of babies from the colony. She disagreed, for had they not lived with *leprosos* all the time? So, as Matilda-i got to know me better, she told me something she had tried out a few years back. It all happened when I was living in the German cottage at another part of the colony, and I did not know anything about it.

She and her husband decided they would risk her having a baby and having it kept by Matilda-i's brother, who lived near the colony. The brother's *compañera* said she would rear the baby along with her own children. Some few months before the baby was born Matilda-i went to visit her brother and stayed there till the baby was born. No one knew about it except her husband. Then she came back to the colony, but she often visited the baby, and that meant being away for a night. Then people began to wonder why she went away so often, and she began to be suspected of infidelity. So she made another arrangement. She persuaded her brother's *compañera* to bring the baby to a lonely part of the boundary, where she could see it.

This plan did not work for long; passers-by had seen her there with the baby and guessed it was hers. When the doctor heard about it, he said it was less risky for the baby to be sent to the preventorium, and she could go there and visit it. So this is what was done. Matilda-i said she had been brokenhearted at the time but now was more at ease about it, as the child was happy and would have more schooling than she had ever had.

**The New Patient**

Matilda-i used to bring me all kinds of news and gossip. One day she brought a newspaper, which someone had given her when she was visiting her child at the preventorium in the big city. It had a full story about a new patient who had just been sent to our colony from a convict settlement, because he had taken leprosy. The story gave all the gossip about him—that he had married a widow with a little girl, and after the widow had died, he had strangled the girl, because she would not consent to his wishes. The story ended up by saying no further punishment, like hard labor, was needed, as banishment to a leprosarium was punishment enough.

This newspaper was passed round all the patients who could read, and they told those who could not read. I felt sorry for the poor man that everyone knew of his sins, for I had come to feel that men are much more harsh than God in their judgments.

The first time I saw this new patient, I saw he was old and bald, and what little hair he had was grey, and he had a sad face. He was standing in the queue. No one spoke to him, and some people moved away from him. When he had gone, there was a burst of chatter. Some patients who came from the same country as he did said they were ashamed to be of the same nationality. Others said, "It gives me the creeps to be standing so near a murderer." But others said, "He looks as if he had confessed and done penance," and yet others said, "He must have suffered enough for it, and perhaps it just was an accident. We have our chaps here, who are put in the *calabozo* for assaults on young girls."

It took some time for folk to get used to seeing him about. Then they got tired of gossiping about him, and they turned their attention to something else.

### Speaking Behind People's Backs

Yes, there is a lot of speaking behind people's backs in the world. I know, because I have done it myself.

It is much easier to speak badly of persons when they are not there. And then if they suddenly come in, just when you are talking badly about them, you can't go on, and then you say, "Oh, come in! I'm so glad to see you," and you say it extra well to them, because you feel bad about how you have been talking. And they know you are saying it extra well and guess that something is wrong; so they do not think you really mean it.

So it's better not to talk badly at all about people, because you couldn't do that if they were there. Then if you always say good things about people, and they suddenly come in, you can say "Come in" properly, and they will feel really welcome, and then you can eat and drink a cup of *maté cocido* ("boiled maté") as friends.

### Don Fidel

The next startling bit of news was the death of poor Don Fidel. No one really knew Don Fidel. He lived alone in a very small hut and kept himself to himself. His nearest neighbors said he did nothing but read books and go out digging for roots of wild plants. Some said he was mad; others said he was only interested in book learning, so was not interested

in us. Others said he was too proud to mix with the likes of us. But I knew
he was not proud. If you greeted him, he always answered you and did
not speak down to you. There were plenty of proud patients. They either
did not speak to you or said a word while looking down their noses at you.
This man was different. He only looked as if he were quite lost in his
thoughts. Folk said he had a belief that the root of a certain *yuyo* ("herb")
could cure leprosy, and he combed the whole area of the colony for it.
Then he crossed the boundary to look for it outside. The poor fellow had
forgotten his face was all nodules and discolored patches, so he was
recognized at once as a *leproso* by a gang of tree-fellers, who killed him
with their machetes.

### Invitation to Don Alfonso's

Another day Matilda-i came to me with quite a different kind of news.
She said she and her sister Piadosa were both invited to the house of Don
Alfonso and Doña Margarita, who were a well-to-do couple and were
important people in the colony. When the doctor was not there, they
walked around the colony with any important visitors who might come.
The reason for the invitation was that Don Alfonso wanted to ask the girls
all they remembered of their early childhood in the colony.

After the visit Matilda-i told me and also everyone else she met about
the grand inside of the house and of the red velvet-covered chairs and sofa
and the fine china and spoons with coffee bean handles, which they used
to stir the sugar in their cups.

But I said, "How did you enjoy the talk you had with them?"

And Matilda-i said, "What a *rompecabeza* ['puzzle' fit to 'break your
head'] all the questions were!" She said she just did not know how to
answer most of the questions. She said there were many things she
couldn't recall, as she was the youngest. Piadosa was the oldest, so she
could answer very many more questions.

"What was the reason for all the questions?" I asked her.

"Oh, I should have told you. Don Alfonso is giving a big talk about
leprosy and about the beginning of the colony here. He is going to speak
from the platform at Alegría [the amusement place]. Will you come with
me?" "Yes," I said, "if I am well enough to walk that day."

Matilda-i called for me on the day of the big talk. She said, "Hurry, I want to get there early." But I said I must tie up my pig first. I had to do this because it followed me about everywhere like a dog.

I never tied up my pig before, until one day at the doctor's office it came in behind me. I had not noticed that it had followed me there. The *enfermera* got into such a rage and shouted, "Take it out, take it out!" and much more besides, which I will not repeat. I don't think the doctor would have been so angry, for he allowed things that gave the patients some interest in life or passed the time for them. And many patients had tame animals besides cats and dogs.

So I tied up my pig and joined Matilda-i.

Doña M.

LH
1959

# Chapter 11: AT THE ALEGRÍA AND
## DON ALFONSO'S SPEECH

**Meeting Friends at the Alegría**

When Matilda-i and I reached Alegría, we found we were quite a bit early for Don Alfonso's talk. But in spite of that a big crowd was there. It looked as if all who could walk or hobble had come.

They were treating each other to drinks at a little booth and toasting each other, but the drinks were non-alcoholic, for the doctor does not allow alcohol. The usual toast was "*Salud y plata* ['health and money'],"
and often someone added, "*Y una novia de yapa* ['and a bride into the bargain'],"  which always raised a burst of laughter.

Matilda-i knew everyone and left me to join this group, or that, of friends or work acquaintances. But I was not long alone. I saw many people I rarely saw.

Anastasia was there, and she greeted me warmly and said, "Doña Maria, why don't you come and visit me?" I got a shock when I saw her; she was so pulled down from the time I lived with her and Eugenio in the first years I was in the colony. She had had to leave Eugenio when the nuns came, as he could not legally marry her. She married later and was there with her husband. I had heard he was often put in the *calabozo* for drinking. Poor fellow—I understood his difficulties when Anastasia said her hands were now so bad that she couldn't work anymore and couldn't even do the washing and cooking for the two of them. "I take all the remedies they give me," she said, "and yet I get worse and worse. I don't understand it, and now it looks as if I will have to lose my fingers." Poor Anastasia—I was so sad for her.

Then Braulia ran up to me and kissed me and said she would never forget how I had trusted her to pay for the calf. She said the calf had turned out to be as good a milker as Mehi and that she was able to sell the milk, which was a great help, for times were bad for musicians in the colony.

111

Then Braulia whispered that she would tell me a secret if I promised not to tell anyone in the colony. She said her brother, Julio, and her husband had got up a trio, with Julio as harpist and her husband and another fellow as guitarists. They had got a friend outside to have horses ready for them, and they had ridden to a village fiesta and played for the dancing and earned some money. Braulia said she and her sister-in-law, Rosita, had dressed the men up so that you would hardly know them, and the friend outside was booking other engagements for them. I then asked Braulia about her mother Felipa. I had lived for a time with Felipa when Braulia and Julio were children. Braulia's face clouded and she said, "Mama can't work now. She stays with Julio and Rosita, or with me and my husband, when she is not in hospital. But each time she goes into the hospital she comes out with a finger or a toe the less."

Just then Martínez came along and sat on a seat on the other side of me, but he didn't see me, for he was lost in listening to the talk of a stranger, who perhaps was a new patient. The stranger was talking away about the *bomba atómica* ("atom bomb"). When there was a pause in the talk, I asked Martínez what kind of bomb that was. Martínez laughed and said, "Most people outside fear it, but if one of them fell on the colony, we would all be cured in a flash!"

### Don Alfonso's Address

Braulia then said, "Hush!" and pointed up the slope, and there were shouts of "*Jaque* ['Watch out']!" as Don Alfonso and Doña Margarita came down the hillside to Alegría with some important visitors.

There was great clapping as they all climbed on to the platform. When the clapping had stopped, Don Alfonso began to speak. He spoke in the Spanish they speak in the cities, so I lost a lot of it.

I also did not take in what he said about the number of *leprosos* in the world and the number in the colony, for I never learnt figures at school. But I remember he said there were twice as many men with leprosy as there were women. He also spoke about all the different remedies that are used for leprosy, but the only name I knew was sulfone.

He then said he had read all he could about leprosy but found the big doctors of the world did not yet know how the infection was picked up. He said he had asked very many patients at the colony if they had any idea of how they had caught leprosy. Two or three of the older patients, who had been in the Bolivia-Paraguay war, blamed the insects in the forest there. They called the forest the "green hell." There were also some campesinos, who had never been in any war, but they also thought it must have come from insects that had bitten someone with the disease before biting them—flies or even *polverinos* (very small flies) perhaps. Others blamed horses or the soil or infected water, and yet others blamed fate. They said, "If you are fated to get leprosy, you will get it."

Then Don Alfonso said he had asked many patients what was the first sign of leprosy they had had. Most people said they had begun to notice they could not feel heat or cold or pain. He himself had first noticed a feeling like ants crawling up his legs, and each time he bent down to knock them off, he found there were none there.

One woman had told him she must have had leprosy years before it was diagnosed. The district where she was born was infested with sand fleas, which lay eggs under the toenail. The eggs grow and cause irritation. She had never felt anything till she saw the swelling with the egg-sac, when it was really big. When she tried to get it out, it broke up her toenail. So most of her toenails remained misshapen. Her brothers and sisters also got sand fleas, but they felt the egg-sac early on and got it out when it was still small, so their toenails were not disfigured like hers.

Then Don Alfonso said we are often asked what is the worst thing we have to suffer as *leprosos*. And he said I am pretty certain most of us would say it is *ostracismo* ("ostracism"), that is that people fear us and shun us and feel safer by having us shut away in leper colonies, and, of course, that means the tragedy of the breakup of the family.

But Don Alfonso said there was hope for us *leprosos*. He said he read everything he could get about the treatment of leprosy in all other parts of the world, and this made him believe a new day would soon dawn, when ostracism and family breakup and leper colonies would be a thing of the past. It would not happen all at once, but it had begun already in some parts of the world.

He said the public must be educated not to fear leprosy. He said we here in the colony know it is not a highly contagious disease. Look at the healthy wives living with husbands who have leprosy, and none of them have taken it, and we even have young women among us, who were born and bred in the colony and yet are free of the disease.

But the public fears and dreads the disease. The dread comes from the terrible words of the ancient Jews, when condemning the *leprosos* to be outcasts "without the camp." That is, they were driven out of the camp or encampment or outside the city wall.

But modern doctors say the disease described in the Old Testament is not leprosy but another skin disease. So the most modern translations of the Bible will not have the words "leper" or "leprosy" in them. Anyway, in the meantime doctors in some parts of the world, like North America, do not use the word "leprosy" at all. They call the disease "Hansen's Disease," because a man called Hansen was the first to discover the bacillus that causes the disease. They also do not use the word "leper," because of the fear both words arouse.

Don Alfonso said there was another law of the ancient Jews, which had had sad consequences for lepers, and that was the law for the purification of someone who had had leprosy and had recovered. Don Alfonso then read these laws out of the Old Testament, in Leviticus 13. The law making a leper into an outcast had these words:

> *And the leper in whom the plague is, his clothes shall be rent, and his head bare, and he shall put a covering over his lips and shall cry "Unclean, unclean!" And all the days wherein the plague shall be in him he shall be defiled, he is unclean, he shall dwell alone, without the camp shall be his habitation.*

Then Don Alfonso read about the ceremony that was used as a law for purification from leprosy. This ceremony confirmed the fact that the leper had recovered from his disease and could be readmitted into the camp (or encampment) or within the city walls and back to his family. The patient, having already been checked and passed as clean by the priest, had now to undergo the purification ceremony. He had to bring two birds to the priest. The priest killed one bird and sprinkled its blood over the other bird and over the patient. Then both the live bird and the man were set at liberty.

The idea of the purifying effect of this "bath of blood" remained throughout the centuries. But people used to think, "The better the blood, the better the cure." So a superstition arose that innocent blood could cure leprosy and that lepers went about looking for babies or innocent young girls in order to bathe in their blood. And this caused more persecution and even killing of lepers.

So far, said Don Alfonso, he had not spoken of the new day, which had already dawned in one part of Brazil, where family breakup and leper colonies were a thing of the past. He said the joy this gave him was immense.

He said that in that part of Brazil a number of jeeps were kept for leprosy doctors, who then were able to cover rough ground to distant parts of the backwoods. Messengers were also sent out to reassure people that if they were found to have leprosy, they would be treated at home and could continue to live with, and support, their families. So no one who feared he had leprosy need go underground, that is, hush up the fact. Every three months the doctor in his jeep would visit the patient and give treatment. At the same time while treating the patient, the doctor would each time check the wife and children for any tiny beginning patch of leprosy. When caught and treated at this early stage, there was a guaranteed cure within a year.

"How different this all is from what many of our older patients have experienced. We have patients here who have told me they had tried to go underground when they first heard they had leprosy." But they had been tracked down and driven at pistol point to the colony, leaving wife or *compañera* and children unsupported, and unchecked for the infection. We also know sad cases, where twenty years later a son or a daughter would arrive, having had undetected and untreated leprosy since babyhood, when the father had been sent to the colony.

### Lázaro

Then Don Alfonso said leprosy had also been called *mal de Lázaro* ("the illness of Lazarus"), because *San Lázaro* ("St. Lazarus") had been cured of leprosy by Jesus.

I did not know which Lazarus he was talking about and would have liked to ask him, but I couldn't interrupt his talk. But afterward for many days I asked a lot of people which Lazarus he meant, and people answered, "Why, the one that had leprosy," and I said, "But which one was that? Was it the brother of Martha and Mary, or was it the beggar who lay at the rich man's gates?" But no one knew, for most of them had never read the Bible.

But the word "*Lázaro*" was well known in the colony. It was used as

a bad word, when someone was angry with someone else and wanted to
call him a bad name. That always started a real fight, for anyone called
"*Lázaro*" was furious and insulted, and sometimes machetes were drawn.
When they cooled down again, I used to chime in and say, "I don't know
why you get so angry when someone calls you '*Lázaro.*' I would not
mind if you called me that. I would be glad. I know two people of that
name in the Bible, and both of them were blessed. One of them was raised
from the dead by Jesus, and the other ended up in Abraham's bosom."
Some folk were interested; others just made big eyes and said nothing.

But I am forgetting Don Alfonso's speech. One of the other things he
said was that it was such a shock when a person was told he had leprosy
that often he became unbalanced and did crazy things. One or two had
even committed murder under the stress, e.g. a young army officer of
high rank, who was engaged to a girl of good family. On the eve of the
wedding he found out that he had leprosy. He was bitterly disappointed
that the girl withdrew from her promise when she heard this, and he
decided no one else should have her. He asked her to go at least for a
good-bye walk with him, and on the walk he killed her. Cases like that are
treated leniently by the judges, who know grief can unhinge the mind,
and no further punishment is considered necessary, as confinement in a
leper colony is considered punishment enough.

Then Don Alfonso said it was not that the colony in itself was a bad
place to be. Indeed, the poor living nearby envied us our assured food
ration, and some came in to share it by marrying patients. But for him, no
good circumstances or conditions could compensate for his loss of
freedom in being confined in a colony.

He said he had found some words written by a *leproso* at the opposite
end of the world, and these words were just what he himself felt in his
heart. I listened carefully and learnt the words by heart. They were: "A
world within the world is a world without the world."

That was the last thing Don Alfonso said. He sat down, and everyone
clapped.

I noticed Martínez and the stranger who was with him liked the words.
They repeated them and nodded with approval. But I did not fully
understand. To me they sounded a bit hopeless, and "without the world"
sounded to me similar to "without the camp" and "outcast," and I thought
no place anywhere is as hopeless and "outcast" as that, for no place is out
of reach of God.

I went home from the talk with these thoughts. Matilda-i stayed on at Alegría after I had left.

# Chapter 12: FAITH AND HOPE VINDICATED

Doña M.

## Inward Peace

When I got home, I made myself a maté and sat in the shade of the creeper by my door and sucked the bombilla Apolinario had given me so many years ago, when I first went to the *reunión*. He had told me the bombilla would be a good *pasatiempo* and would mix well with my thoughts.

Now, as I had to sit so much, I found it a fine pastime. In my more active days I did not linger for hours with my maté bombilla, but I always liked maté. I found it warmed you when you were cold and cooled you when you were hot, and it gave you fresh energy when you were tired.

And I found now that it was truer than ever that the bombilla mixed well with my thoughts. But I found my thoughts had completely changed since those early days in the colony. Then my thoughts were entirely about me or about mine. I was sorry for myself, and it was always a case of "poor me," and I worried endlessly about my husband and my son.

Now I hardly ever thought about myself. I often used to think I had little more education than one of my hens, but I knew that just as God had cared for me all these years, so he could care for my husband and child also. So I did not worry anymore but trusted them to His hands, for I knew He could care for them better than I could.

And I began to realize how many things I would not have known if I had stayed happily at home, with husband, son, house, and farm, and kith and kin nearby. For at the colony I was forced to find strength and comfort in the Bible and the hymnal.

I had also learnt that God can come and give a joy such as I had never heard of when I had all the things around me that folk prize most in life— husband, child, and home.

**Right Answers Provided**

Also I found that somehow the right answer came to me, when I was placed in an awkward position. Once I arrived at the very end of a long queue for stores. A woman in the queue, who is married to an important man in the colony, shouted to me, "Ah, Doña Maria, you are late, because you spend so much time reading that Bible of yours."

A verse out of a hymn came into my mind, and I said it:

*Santa Biblia, para mí eres un tesoro aquí.*
*Tú contienes con verdad la divina voluntad.*
["Holy Bible, thou art a treasure for me here;
thou containest in truth the divine will."]

Everyone laughed, and ever since this grand lady smiles at me and says, "Ah, Doña Maria, have you anything else interesting for me today?"

Another time, I was among a crowd of women at the hospital. They were all dressed in their Sunday best, and all were excited over the *fiesta de San Juan*. A nun asked me, "How is it, Doña Maria, that you are the only one who does not take part?"

I answered with a line from another hymn. I sang it: "*Yo dejo al mundo y su vana pompa* ['I leave the world and its vain pomp']." No one was offended, and one or two came and asked me afterwards about my religion.

## Distressing Insights

My eyes were also opened to see many things I had never seen before. I used to watch the big public funerals go by with their long processions, and I saw how the whole procession stopped now and then to recite prayers. But I noticed that they only stopped where there was a cluster of houses, and not in between where there were no houses and where only God would hear.

And I used to watch the vultures gather around a dying cow on the campo. They always made a circle round the animal with their wings spread out, and then they would fix their eyes on the sky, as if they were all praying, but all the time they were waiting for the cow to die.

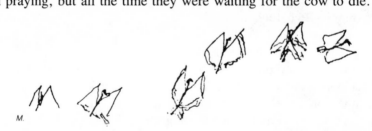

And I saw the same thing among men, where folk used to come round to visit a very ill person, but all the time they were looking to see where he kept his money or his watch. I have seen a table disappear out of a man's house the minute he had drawn his last breath.

## God Can Do What Seems Impossible

But though I have seen so many hardhearted things, I have not lost hope, for I know God can do what seems impossible to us. He never uses force on people, but in His own way He can change men's hearts through His Spirit. And His Spirit acts in many unseen ways.

I had proof of this one day, when I suddenly got word that an airplane was coming to take me to get my big operation done. My husband had spoken to some folk, and God had spoken to their hearts, and so they had offered to do the operation free of charge and sent an airplane to fetch me.

I had never been out of the colony for eighteen years, since I had come in on a wagon, and here I was flying out like a bird! I never thought I would live to have a flight in a plane. I looked out of the window and saw the folk in the colony like ants crawling among the *yuyos*.

And I thought, "That is what we must look like to God, and I am just one of those ants, and I have done nothing to arrange it, yet here I am flying out, because God has worked in the hearts of some strangers. For God is compassion and love."

*Doña M.*

*Doña M.*

E.B.

# Part 3:

## GOD IS OVER ALL

**More "Parables From the Underworld"**
**as Recorded by Maureen Burn and Belinda Manley, 1954-1958**

## How I Got to Know Maria at Primavera

The first time I saw Maria was from the laboratory window at Primavera Hospital. One of our doctors told me our patient from the Santa Isabel Colony would be arriving any time now, and she was going down to our air strip to meet the little plane bringing her. She asked me to go to the isolation hut as soon as the patient had settled in, and take some blood for tests.

I knew Maria had been separated from her husband and son for eighteen years, so I expected to see a broken-down, sad-looking woman. However, from my window I was surprised to see a rather thin but lively person, looking round her as she sat beside our doctor on a wagon driven by one of our brothers. The wagon passed on to the isolation hut, and I got my equipment ready.

In her hut, Maria gave me a smiling welcome and laughed when I said I had come to take a little blood from her. She talked away quite freely in Spanish, and when there was a word I did not understand, I asked her. Then I said she could be my teacher in Spanish, as I did not know it so well. At that she had a hearty laugh and said she could teach no one anything; she was a *tonta*.

Four days later, on July 12, 1954, she underwent a successful operation in our hospital, and then she spent eighteen months living in her little isolation hut near the hospital.

She was desperately lonely there. If I visited her for a few minutes at morning snack, she always said, "I do hope God sends you tonight." How glad I would have been if others could visit more often. But most of them had young children, and those without children usually could not speak Spanish, which was Maria's chief language.

She had been advised rest and treatment, but it was very difficult to keep her inactive for long. She used to go out with a hoe and extend the little garden round the isolation hut. All kinds of flowers started to bloom. She said they were from seeds her son had sent.

Then small bushes of gardenias and hibiscus started to appear. When asked if these also came from her son's seeds, she laughed and said, "Oh no, those were flowers given me for my vase, and later I planted the twigs," and pointing to a row of tomato plants she said, "And those came from a bad tomato I had in my dinner."

On the return journey from the Santa Isabel Colony, toward the end of 1955, we took Maria to see two leprosy specialists in Asuncion, and they pronounced her a "burnt-out case." One was a world-famous man, who was visiting Asuncion at the time. They said she was symptom-free and that her husband and son could join her. When Maria heard this, she beamed and said, "God is over all!"

### Bueno

I came to visit Maria and she said, "One day when I was lying in bed after my operation, one of the brothers came to see me. He told me I could stay here in the community, if I liked. So I said, '*Bueno* ["good"].'

"Later I thought: All my friends are in Sapucay. There they would often come in to see me, and because they all had the disease too, they were not afraid; they would sit on one of my chairs and not mind. Then I thought: Perhaps here people would be too afraid to come and see me.

"Again I thought: There it was difficult to find enough to eat. Everyone was out for themselves. Here all share, and there is enough for all.

"I am ill too, I thought, and here there are doctors. If I got ill there in the colony, I had to go to the women's hospital, where everyone bosses you and tells you what to do.

"So I thought and thought and couldn't sleep. I didn't know what to do. Then I thought: *Bueno*, I don't know, but God knows what He wants to do with me. Then everything was quiet in me, and I stayed."

### Not Alone Anymore

One day I visited Maria. She was in bed. Her feet had been troubling her, and she was resting them.

"I am a bad patient," she said. "I find it hard not to be able to go out and work in the garden. And then I think of Apolinario. He can't work anymore. He can't read anymore. But he is always cheerful. People go to him to get cheered up if they are down."

She paused and then she continued again, "I heard the priest once looked in to see Apolinario, because he was sorry for him living all alone. The priest asked him why he did not move into the hospital, where he would have company and nursing care.

"'Thank you for your kindly thought,' said Apolinario, 'but I am not alone.'

"The priest looked round the little room to see if anyone else was there.

"'No, you will not see anyone, but I feel the presence of God. You could say there's four of us here: the Father, the Son, and the Spirit—all in the Presence!'"

**Watch and Pray**

Maria was reading slowly from a book as I approached her cottage. "Hello, Maria!" I called out.

"Ah, hello!" she replied, "I was afraid no one was coming to see me today. Come and sit down."

"What are you reading?" I asked.

"All about holding fast to what Jesus can do for us," she replied. "But now you've come, let's read about the devil and how he tries to catch us."

She laughed. "He's such a crafty one that we must always watch out. What does it say in the Bible? Yes: Watch and pray! That's what we must do—pray, because he always tries to catch us again and again, and we can't get around him alone. We must pray. Then God will answer us, and He will always win.

"Now we'll read how he tries to catch us each day—see, here it says it: Watch and pray!"

Doña M.

## God Knows All

It was a fine, sunny morning, and I was out for a walk with the preschool children. I said to them, "We are quite near Maria's house. She has to be there all alone, because she is ill. Shall we go to the bottom of her garden and sing some morning songs?"

They were very pleased at the idea, but, because children can catch the disease more easily, I was not able to take them up to Maria's hut but left them there, singing of sunflowers and animals, and went up the garden path to fetch Maria out of her room. She came out very happy to be visited, and we both stood together listening to the children.

I watched her face. Slowly she became very thoughtful, and then, with a sad look on her face, she turned to me and, indicating a fair-haired boy standing in front, said, "My boy was just his age when we had to separate. But I say to myself: God knows it all. He can look after my boy and my husband better than I can. He knows it all, and maybe He will make it all come right one day."

**The End of the World**

Maria loved it when someone went and read to her in the evening out of her Spanish Bible or out of some Baptist periodicals she was given.

One evening I was reading to her out of a periodical, where the Jehovah's Witnesses were mentioned. That awakened a chain of memories in Maria, and she would interrupt the reading to share what was on her mind. I liked the fresh spontaneity in her, especially as her anecdotes were deeply based and rooted in her faith.

"Oh," said Maria, "not so long ago one of the *sanas* at the colony returned from a visit to her parents outside, and she was trembling. I asked her what was the matter and she said, 'The end of the world— soon—it's terrible! A lot of people believe it, also my mother.'

"I said to her, 'Don't upset yourself, Lola! No one knows when the end of the world will be, not even Jesus. He said He didn't know, nor did the angels know, but only God knows. All you have to do is to watch and pray and live the best way you can.'

" 'Oh, is that really true?' said Lola.

" 'Yes, it is true; it is written in the Scriptures,' said I.

" 'Then I won't be worried,' said Lola."

Maria turned to me and said, "When I was young like Lola, there was a great scare about the end of the world. I was working at a corned beef factory to make some money, for my father's *chacra* barely supported us. Some Jehovah's Witnesses came and made great propaganda. My parents had heard exactly the same thing when I was a baby in Bavaria, so I didn't take much notice. Anyway, I was too occupied with dress and amusements at the time. But many girls at the factory stopped working. They said, 'What is the good of making more money if the world is going to end any time soon.' Others gave away their dresses or gave their wages to beggars on the streets, for they said, 'It is better to lay up treasure in Heaven for later on.'

"Others continued working at the factory, but every now and then they would go out and look up at the sky to see if they saw any signs of the end coming. But I just laughed and thought they had a screw loose, and in the end they got tired of waiting and went back to the worldly life I was living. In later years I would often wonder how all that kind of excitement and panic could arise, but I had no answer. It was only after I had learned the truth that man does not live by bread alone that I knew men are open to believe any rumor, however far-fetched, if they do not live by every word that comes from the mouth of God."

## God Never Forces

I was reading to Maria out of *Pilgrim's Progress*, and we had just reached the part where Christian's heavy burden fell off his back and rolled away, when he came to the foot of the Cross. Here Maria broke in with a flood of reminiscences.

"Yes," she said, "I know what it is like to carry a heavy burden, and I carried it for a long, long time—it must have been many years—for God never forces us." She had a suck at her bombilla, and I saw she was gathering her distant memories. Then she continued, "Because God never forces us to the foot of the Cross, and indeed that is the last place that man in his pride will go to.

"I first realized I had this heavy burden on my back when I was living by myself in a little hut on our family *chacra*. I was there two years. At first I worried about my illness and because I might be sent away to a place that would be like being put in the grave. But as time went by, I got beyond that kind of worry, and I began to think, 'If it is leprosy, it will pass with the body, but what about my soul?' And I thought of my frivolous twenties and my vanity and dancing, and I would think, 'I must surely belong to the devil.'

"There was a tin of weedkiller in my hut with the picture of a devil on it. It frightened me, and I hid it. People thought I was mad worrying about my soul now, instead of my body. They brought a Salvation Army man to talk to me. He said, 'We are all sinners, but we don't know it. Jesus came for sinners. He is the Savior, and there is no one He cannot save.'

"I heard the words the man spoke, but they did not mean anything to me. I was too dulled by depression. Later, in the leper colony, my ears became even duller, so that I no longer believed in either God or the devil. I just wanted to die and end the misery of pining for what I had lost in husband, child, and home.

"It was only years later that I began to turn freely to God, and I learnt the meaning of the words the man had spoken to me so long before. And I learnt that God never forces folk. He waits years in patience for man's free-willing love. That is why I love to sing '*Tú dejaste tu trono y corona para mí* ["Thou didst leave Thy throne and crown for me"].'"

**Jesus the Savior**

"Now I'll get my songbook," said Maria, "and we'll sing of Jesus the Savior. There are many songs that say '*Jesús salvador*' in my book. He came to save people and especially the bad, wicked ones. The good and the proud folk say, 'We're all right.' But those who know they have been so bad and wicked that they can't help themselves can only say, 'Help me, Lord,' and He does. So He is the Savior."

And she laughed and said, "I have to say that, and then He does help me every time. Now listen! Here it says it," and she read me one of her songs.

*Cristo mí salvador resucitó, resucitó, resucitó;*
*Cristo mi salvador resucitó; siempre conmigo está.*
["Christ my Savior is risen, risen, risen;
Christ my Savior is risen and is always with me."]

**Sing From the Heart**

Maria loved singing *himnos celestiales* ("spiritual hymns"). She said they were like prayers and uplifted her. I managed to learn to sing two of them with her. One of them was "*Tú dejaste tu trono*," which I have mentioned already. The other was "*Gracia, paz y perdón consigue el pecador* ['Grace, peace, and forgiveness are granted to the sinner']."

She sings slowly, and if she stumbles over a word, she repeats it rightly. She said that in the little Sunday morning meeting at Apolinario's they loved singing songs out of the little Salvation Army hymn book. Apolinario used to say, "Sing from the heart and in faith, believing the words. The tune is less important."

"That is what I believe," she said. "I sing as it comes out of the heart, without bothering if the note is just the right one or not. We all sang like that at Apolinario's. None of us would have opened our mouths if we had to get the right note every time. But some folk say, 'No, no, it is not that

Doña M.

note!" and they point to a note in a book and say, 'It is this note!' and they tap the table to make us hurry up. I'm no good for that kind of singing, and it makes me sad. Then I think, 'But the birds sing to God, and they don't need a book with notes in it.'"

## To Be a Brother

Maria had two different songbooks from two different groups of people, the Salvation Army and the Baptists. She was always pleased when she found the same songs had been sung in each of the groups. She said to me, "Sometimes the words are a bit different, but the meaning is the same. Look, here in this book it speaks of 'brothers of the Lord,' and in the other book it speaks of 'soldiers of the Lord.' But it's the same, because you have to fight to be a brother to the Lord—not with the things they use in wars, but you have to fight your own self. That means not to be proud and think you're the best at anything, and not to decide what you want to do, but just to let God tell you."

## The Crucified Thieves

Someone gave Maria a copy of Papini's *Life of Christ*, and she told me she liked the passage about the two thieves who were crucified with Jesus. Then she retold in her own words what she had read, "One of the thieves mocked Jesus just as the Pharisees were doing. He said, 'If you are really the Christ, come down from the Cross and save yourself and us too.' He thought he would win the approval of the crowd by siding with them, and then perhaps they would set him free. He was still just thinking of his body and his present life."

She paused and then continued about the other thief. "The other thief believed Jesus was the Christ. He said, 'Lord, remember me when you come into your Kingdom,' and Jesus accepted him.

"It is a most wonderful thing—that forgiveness of Jesus—like a flash! Men would have said the thief needed more time to repent properly or to better himself. But Jesus said, 'This day shalt thou be with me in Paradise.'"

**Papini's** *Life of Christ*

Someone had told Maria that Papini had been a Roman Catholic when he wrote his book, and probably still was one. She was delighted to hear that. I asked her why, and she said, "It's just the book to give to Catholics, and they won't be afraid to read it. I wish I had had it when I was in the colony. I would have lent it to Catholics who could read. Everything in the book is true, and he does not mention images or the Pope or mass.

"It just shows how wrong it is of us to judge others because we don't like something in their religion. In spite of that, the Spirit of God can live in them. Just look at Francis of Assisi. He was a Roman Catholic, yet he was one of the most Christlike of men.

"It also shows that the name of the religion or the outer forms or beliefs are not the important thing. The important thing is the Spirit, and no matter what the cult is, those who have the Spirit of the Lord are the Lord's. And the Spirit alone knows who are its own children."

**The Forest Iris**

Maria had made a nice little flower garden in front of her hut and was glad of any roots or cuttings for it. I found some nice wild forest irises and dug up a few for her. Our botanist-pharmacist saw them and said, "It's funny, those flowers have two completely opposite names in Spanish. One is *flor del diablo* ['devil's flower'] and the other is *lágrimas de María* ['tears of Mary']." I repeated all this to Maria, but she declared, "The names are not different. It is the devil who causes the tears of Mary." "How?" said I. "Well," she said, "He makes people worship her rather than her Son."

**Birds Are Free of Passports**

We had two or three Mennonite nurses doing voluntary work at our Primavera hospital. One day one of these was talking to Maria when I came up to visit her.

"Well, well," Maria said to her, "so you can't go and visit your mother in that country, because you don't have the right papers? I'm sorry about that. But could you not sell all your things and pay an airplane to fly you over the border somewhere?"

"No," said the nurse, "wherever a plane lands, they ask for papers."

"Well, well," said Maria, "that is just the way of man in his pride. They want to be lords of the earth, and whenever a plane touches the earth, it is at once under their rules and regulations again. So it seems that a plane is only free like a bird so long as it is in the air. It is as though man had quite forgotten that God is over all."

### The Tropical Thunderstorm

One morning I went up to visit Maria. The footpath was a muddy stream; the long grass at either side was soaking wet, and the wind blew big drops of water off the trees onto my face. It was the morning after a tropical thunderstorm.

After greeting me, Maria laughed and said, "I felt as if I were in a camion (truck) last night. The whole room shook, and I could see the lightning through my closed eyelids. And what a noise the thunder made! I was thinking of all the people who say, '*Yo soy yo* ["I am I"], and there is nothing more.' And I thought men are so puffed up with their own power, but even a thunderstorm should remind them there is more power above than there is below, on earth."

### God Knows My Goings-out and My Comings-in

Maria was a real country woman. She was happiest with a hoe in her hands, or caring for animals. After a light fall of rain, when the ground was less hard, she would be busy outside her hut in Primavera. She hoed many patches of wild land and planted maize. She would keep a good cob of maize with big grains for this purpose. Then she used to water it, faithfully carrying buckets of water from a tap.

One night she heard a thunder of hoofs passing her window. She knew it was horses. She went out next morning and found her corn patch ruined. She examined the hoof marks and found it was three horses that had done it. Nothing daunted, she planted another patch and yet another

Doña M.

patch, and each time the horses came and did the same thing.

She told me that horses have a real mania for juicy growing corn, and if they are not well paddocked at night, they will somehow break out to get it. When the last patch had gone, she said, *"Bueno,* I think God must have sent those three horses all those times, for He must have known that Otto [the brother looking after the pigs in Primavera] needs help with his pigs." So she went to Otto, and he was very glad when she offered to prepare and boil the food for the pigs.

She did this for a couple of months, and then her feet began to trouble her again, and the doctor ordered bed.

Maria so enjoyed an active out-of-doors life that I thought she would be disappointed, but not a bit of it! When I went up to visit her, I found her reading in bed, and she said with a smile, "It seems God wants me to read His Word, so He has arranged it that I must stay in bed." And she laughed.

## God Gives Everything

Maria said, "I know you all give up everything here, when you want to live together, and some were rich and brought a lot, and some brought less, but what about me? I've got nothing to give, because I've brought nothing—only trouble for the hospital!" She laughed. "So I say to myself: What can I give them?"

"Well, you do give us a lot of joy, Maria," I said, "because you always have something to say or sing or laugh about, when we come to see you."

"Well, I do have hard days too," said Maria. "When it rains or my feet are bad, and I can't go out to work with the pigs. Then I think: Now I had better read the Bible; so I do, and then I sing a bit, and God makes me glad again. So you see God gives everything. So what have I to give? Nothing at all!"

**The Lamb of God That Takes Away the Sin of the World**

It was very hot, and the cicadas were singing so loudly that I could hardly hear what Maria was saying. (The children in Primavera used to say that Christmas is near when the cicadas make a big noise.)

Maria had brought two chairs out in front of her door. It was cooler there than indoors. She then asked me to read the story of the birth of Jesus, and so I did. In the Spanish Bible the word "*mesón*" is used for "inn." "*Mesón*" must be an obsolete word, for Maria had never heard it. She stopped me when I got to the bit about there being no room in the inn, and she said, "*Mesón* means maternity hospital, doesn't it?" "Oh no," I said, "it is a hostel or an inn."

"Oh," she said, "I never knew that. I thought that God had arranged it that the maternity home was too full, so that Mary had to go to a cattle shed so that Jesus Christ should be born among sacrificial animals, to show that He was to take their place and sacrifice His life for men."

**The Red Party (Conservative) and the Blue Party (Liberal)**

At the Primavera hospital patients' relatives stayed with the patients if they had come from a distance, so Aubrelina was left by her parents to stay with her small sister, who was ill. One day Aubrelina went up to Maria and asked if she could pick some of Maria's flowers. "Yes, of course," said Maria. "I am always glad if people can use my flowers. Then I feel I have not planted them for nothing." Then Maria pointed out to Aubrelina which flowers were just right for picking. Then she added, "Oh, and over there, there are some half-opened buds on that rosebush. They will open in a day or two and have a lovely perfume. They are beautiful red roses." "Oh no," said the girl, "I couldn't take those. My parents belong to the Blue Party. If they saw red flowers picked for them, they would throw them away. They are coming to visit today."

"But that's foolish," said Maria to the girl. "God made all the flowers and the red ones too. And surely the blood of Jesus was red also."

**Only God Is Not Blind**

One day Maria said, "Here are a lot of things I don't understand."
"What do you mean?" I asked.
She sucked away at her bombilla, and I knew she was trying to find words to express what she was feeling.
"Well," she said, "because of what I have suffered and learnt in the leper colony, I am a great believer in preaching the Gospel. The people who live in Christian community and brotherhood do not always understand this, and so I am sometimes tempted to think they are blind on this point. But then, I know for sure that there are even more things that I am blind to."
"What for instance?" I asked.
"Well," she said, "I don't understand what leads to war and peace, and I don't understand what leads to riches and poverty, and there are many more things that they know about and I don't know about and which they say are part of the Gospel. And then I think, 'Everyone is blind on something. Only God is not blind and knows all.'"

**God's Garden Tools**

One day Maria showed me a Salvation Army paper. It was the German version of the *War Cry*. I asked her where she had got it, and she replied, "Oh, a German lady brought it to me. I thanked her but said I could only read in Spanish, not German, and I asked her if she would read some of it to me, but she wasn't very willing. I asked her, 'Don't you like it?' and she answered, 'Those people speak too openly about sacred things.'

'Yes,' I said, 'some of them get people's backs up. They ask right out, "Are you saved?" But there are others who are quite different.'

"'But none of them live in brotherhood,' said she.

"'No,' I said, 'but they feel called to go out and seek the lost. Some of God's instruments are used for sowing and others for gathering in. He needs all kinds of tools for His harvest. He does not work only with a machete. He also needs spades and hoes and *cuchillas finas* ["fine knives for pruning"].'"

### How Maria Wanted Me to Go With Her to Santa Isabel

Toward the end of 1955 Maria was expecting to go back to the leper colony, to take leave of her friends, settle up her affairs and return to Primavera. She said to me, "I would be so glad if you could come with me, Morin [Maureen]."

"I would love to go," said I, "but I will have to ask." Nothing could have given me greater joy than being able to accompany her. For I had been so inspired by Maria's triumphant faith that I wanted to meet one or two at Santa Isabel who had inspired her. I felt that a faith in Christ like that was of desperate importance whether living in community like us, or outside. I wished for it—above all else for my family. I also felt that only by meeting these people could I write something, which I had an inner urge to do.

Then unfortunately I took flu. Some days later I had a relapse, because I came back to work too soon, and then I had a heart attack as well and had to be carried to the hospital on a stretcher. I felt all right next day but was not allowed up for a week. It seemed that I might not be able to accompany her, but Maria never gave up hope. One day she even ventured to walk down to the hospital from her isolation hut and inquired where I was lying and waved to me through the window to encourage me. Else Boller, who looked after Maria's clothes, told me that when she went to take Maria her washing or the mending she did for her, Maria had said to her, "Do you know if Morin is asking to go with me?"

"Yes," said Else, "she asked the Brotherhood."

"Oh, I don't mean that; she told me that. I mean: Do you know if Morin is asking God about it? God is over the Brotherhood!"

## The Pumpkin Seed, or the Sower

After we got back from settling up Maria's affairs at the leper colony, I visited her one day, and she put a seed into my hand. She was just delighted to have it and fondled it carefully. Then she said, "When we were at Sapucay, I had hoped to get some seeds of a special kind that they have there but you don't have here. But I was told there had been a real shortage of hen food, and the seeds had all been given to the hens. I was so sorry—it's a pumpkin with a wonderful taste, not just insipid like the usual ones.

"Then when I was looking for a button in my button box, I found one among the buttons. Maybe it's been there for years; I never remember putting it in. I'm going out to plant it and water it and watch it grow, and I'll keep seeds from it to give you for the vegetable garden here."

"That's a wonderful find; I'm so pleased," said I.

Then she continued, "That seed made me think of the parable of the sower. Many believers keep their seed safe and dead, like mine in a button box, yet it should be sown, in word and in deed, and then it will bring forth fruit."

"Yes," she said, "the Word should be preached to people who have never heard it. There will come a day when they will be asked, 'Why did you do that?' and they will answer, 'Well, we didn't know any other way; you can't blame us, Lord. Nobody told us.'"

She had a good, long suck at her bombilla, and then she added, "But there is a way of 'sowing' that closes the hearts of the hearers. That is when we are superior and harsh like the Pharisees. And there is a way of 'sowing' that opens the heart. That is when it is done in love and humility. But we are all called to sow the seed we have."

## Feeding People

"I'll read to you about feeding people," said Maria to me last Sunday. "It says that when Christ asked the disciples to give the bread out among all those people who were hungry, they should first give it to *Him*, and then He would break it into pieces and give it back to them, to give to the people. First though it must be given to Him! You see what it says: first to Him!

"That's like preaching, telling people about the Bread of Life. First one must go to Christ; one must have the right center. Then when He says, one can go and tell people. But first it must always be that one goes to Christ."

## Preachers

One day I was telling Maria my nephew had decided to become a clergyman.

"What do you think of that, Maria?" I asked.

"You mean he wants to become a preacher?" she asked.

"Yes, he will preach, no doubt," I said, "and of course do other things."

"*Bueno*," she said and mixed her yerba (maté) with boiling water and began to suck it. I thought she had forgotten my question. Then suddenly she said, "*Bueno*, if God has told him to preach, that is all right, but if he himself has said, 'I will be a preacher,' that is wrong. Then it will be the 'I' that is preaching, and that will be no good. For only God has something to say to men, and He will tell those whom He wants to preach, and He will tell them what to say."

## God Exalts and God Humbles, God Parts and God Unites

At the end of August 1956 a message came through on the radio linking Primavera with our community house in Asuncion saying that, after many years of separation, Maria's husband was coming from our community in Uruguay to join her in Primavera. I went up at once to Maria to tell her the good news. She was busy reading the Bible, and before I had time to say anything, she smiled and said, "I am reading about Nebuchadnezzar, who had to learn to be humble by eating grass with the cattle."

Then I told her the news. She put her Bible down and said, "God exalts and God humbles; He parts and He unites."

**Wristwatches**

Maria was given nice, roomy quarters near where I lived, when her husband joined her. They also had a nice garden area with an outdoor table and seats. I had to pass by, going to or returning from work, and Maria always hailed me and asked me to spend at least a few minutes with her.

One morning we got straight into a topic that concerned me very much, so I wanted to hear what she had to say about it and stayed longer than I had intended. Then I remembered my work and said, "Some people may look at their watches and then at me, when I get up to the hospital." "Oh," answered Maria, "the most important things have nothing to do with clocks. Jesus made use of any opening to say or do what God put in His heart, and didn't He praise Mary rather than Martha? And I never heard that He ever had a wristwatch."

**The Thief and the Gold Watch**

I was going home early from work when I passed Maria's husband working in the vegetable garden. He greeted me and said she would be glad if I visited. So I went there.

Maria asked me to read to her. I picked up a Baptist periodical and began to read. It was a little sermonette on the power of a bad habit.

> One day a parson was visiting in a hospital, and the matron pointed to a badly wounded man, who had been robbing a jeweller's shop. The parson said, "Shall I pray for you?" The thief nodded. Then the parson knelt by the bedside and shut his eyes and prayed. When the prayer was over, the man was dead, and clutched in his fingers was the parson's gold watch.

"Oh," exclaimed Maria, "I hope when I come to die that I shall be thinking of God and not of gold."

Her answer to the little story bypassed all moralism and went to the very heart of the matter.

### The Abbé Pierre Movement

As Maria's husband was very deaf, he could not give a whispered translation into Spanish to Maria in meetings conducted in English or German. I was one of the people who did that for her. But one day I thought I would have a rest from it. So I said to her, "G. has the meeting today. He uses simple German and speaks slowly. Do you think you will understand?" "I think so," she said.

We had all heard about the Abbé Pierre movement, and this evening a couple of young German helpers, who worked in the Buenos Aires branch of the movement, were with us. G. commented on all the helpful service they did in housing the homeless from the proceeds of junk sorting. "But," he said, "good! That is outer help, but how is it with inner help?" Much was said on this theme, and I saw Maria with her "tree trunk look." That meant she did not understand. So I whispered, What did she not understand? And she said, "I can't understand why those nice people won't help inside the houses of the poor, but only outside."

"No, that is not it," I said. "Outer help" is to give housing, clothes, and food to the people, and "inner help" is to talk about God."

"Why doesn't G. say that then?" said she.

### Sunlight Knowledge and Moonlight Knowledge

Another day, I was translating in a meeting for Maria. It was about our new Bruderhof in North America—*América del Norte* in Spanish. She whispered to me, "This is *América del Norte*, isn't it?" (We were, of course, in South America.) I then realized how completely lacking she was in the most rudimentary schooling.

She had never seen a map and knew nothing of geography. She had never learned to write or do figures. If ever she had wanted to sell a calf, for example, she had to turn to a friend and trustfully accept the change that was given back to her when buying anything herself. She told me she had learnt the letters and could spell three-lettered words by the time she had to leave school. It was only many years later that she really began to read in order to read the Bible. And yet anyone who visited her in the mid-1950s, as I did, came away enriched.

I thought of George Fox and the early Quakers. As Fox traveled up and down England, he was heard with interest everywhere, except at Oxford and Cambridge. These were the only two university towns in England at that time. Someone commented to Fox that it was strange that the learned college folk did not respond more to his message. "No," said Fox, "it's not strange, because wherever men concentrate on the 'moonlight knowledge' of the intellect, they run the danger of missing the 'sunlight knowledge' of inward illumination by God."

Doña M.

# EPILOGUE

Back at Primavera after our return from Santa Isabel, I scribbled an account of all we had experienced on our journey. This account lay for twenty-three years, till Kathleen, my sister, found it among papers I was going to throw out. She deciphered the yellowing, scribbled pages and typed them. Slightly shortened, they form the first part of this book.

My urge had been to write down something of what Maria had shared with me. In the foregoing stories I changed the names of nearly all the people, so as to hide their identity and not cause offense or occasion gossip. Now, however, several decades have passed since I lived in Paraguay and knew these people, who now, like myself, will be well beyond the allotted three score years and ten, if indeed they are still alive. So I will mention the real name of one of the men about whom I wrote. It is Ambrosio Castillo. I changed it to Apolinario Caceres when I wrote about him.

In Primavera, when Maria told me her life story (bit by bit over several years), she always spoke of him as the one who held together the few Protestants at the Santa Isabel leprosarium during the years of discrimination against Protestants. A few years after Maria left the leper colony, the benign influence of Pope John XXIII caused the removal of much of this discrimination, and Salvation Army officers could again visit Ambrosio and his small group. But when I went with Maria and Peter Mathis to Santa Isabel late in 1955, the Salvation Army was not welcome in the colony. On the way there, while we were in Asuncion, Maria asked me to call at the Salvation Army headquarters and ask them if they would like to write some letters to Ambrosio Castillo and his group, who were so cut off, as no visits were allowed from Protestant pastors or Evangelical preachers.

149

When I passed this message on to the district officer there, Mrs. Major
Joseph Diaz, she became very excited and said, "Ambrosio Castillo? I
met him twenty years ago, when he was a wounded soldier and I was
giving out literature. Yes, we will leave parcels and letters tonight at the
Bruderhof House in Asuncion."

When on our return journey from Santa Isabel we took to the Salvation
Army headquarters the letters Ambrosio had entrusted to us, Mrs. Diaz
was most interested to hear about our meeting with Ambrosio. She was
the very same Salvation Army "lassie" who had first spoken to Ambrosio
in 1936.

Some years later I visited a Salvation Army meeting in Canterbury,
England, with a friend, and I was asked to tell about the Salvation Army
in Paraguay. I decided to tell about Ambrosio Castillo. Some time later I
received from my friend a copy of the All the World magazine, dated
October 1965. In it were two articles supplied by Captain Robert Gurney
of the Salvation Army, with photos of Ambrosio Castillo and his little
hut. This is the first article, headed:


## ISOLATED BY LEPROSY

"It's a three-hour journey by bullock cart from the station, or
two hours' walk," said the District Officer to the Territorial
Commander, Colonel Hjalmar Eliasen. "Oh, we're quite prepared
to walk," he replied, speaking for himself and the Chief Secretary,
"we must get there somehow and see if we can do anything. We
would like to hold a meeting also, if possible." Their destination
was the leprosarium of Sapucay, Paraguay, where seventy-year-old
Sergeant Castillo lives in a small thatched hut that has been his
home since 1936.

When Colonel Eliasen and Lieut.-Colonel Johannes Clausen
visited Paraguay recently, they were, as usual, ready for anything.
Eventually, neither the bullock cart nor the two-hour walk was
necessary, as the District Officer, Major Mario Jourdan, was able to
hire an air-taxi, which took them directly to the leprosarium without
any difficulties.

The eighty-kilometer flight saw them leave Asuncion and head south over the interminable jungles of Paraguay, until, with even the pilot beginning to doubt that he could find his way, they eventually began to descend on to what is little more than a small clearing in the undergrowth—the landing strip.

They had arrived at the Santa Isabel leprosy settlement, Sapucay, where live some 300 families, cut off from the outside world, and scattered over a large area of land, which is really no more than jungle. Whilst the work there comes under the Government, as in all hospitals in the country, nuns of the Roman Catholic faith are in charge; at the present time the director is a Franciscan monk. Apart from the 300 family dwelling-places there are two large pavilions, one for men, the other for women.

Since his admittance to the settlement twenty-eight years ago, the valiant Sergeant Castillo has been holding his own meetings, in Salvationist fashion, with a regular congregation of some fifteen to twenty persons. He finds no hindrance from the authorities, who gave a warm welcome to the Territorial Commander. As an example of the recognition given by them, the director chose a Salvationist to guard the stores when it was discovered that things were disappearing!

Sergeant Castillo is now blind and has been given a young lad to help him about the place. This boy acts as his eyes and runs the errands necessary to keep body and soul together, maintaining the plot of land, from which the majority of their food is obtained. There are one or two cooperatives, where a little meat or a few extra things can be bought. Colonel Eliasen was able, during his visit, to arrange for the Sergeant to buy something each week, making the [Salvation] Army responsible for the payment.

Living is precarious: a constant fight to keep the undergrowth from covering the food plot and a little bargaining here and there to make enough money with which to buy that little extra. The Sergeant's hut is practically empty, containing nothing that we would think of as being home, but here for so many years he has carried on his faithful ministry. His blue uniform has been bleached by the constant sun to a mauve colour, and the braid is almost red. So moved was the assistant officer in Asuncion when he visited the place that he left his own Army cap, so as to complete the Sergeant's uniform.

The only contact maintained with the outside world is by means of radio, and when the batteries run out, it sometimes means a long wait before someone arrives with replacements. No newspapers reach Sapucay, although now with the lifting of some of the restrictions of movement the [Salvation] Army's fortnightly edition of *El Cruzado* ["The Crusader"] is received—with much appreciation.

The second article, headed "Sergeant Castillo," included a brief account by Mrs. Brigadier Joseph Diaz, who had first met Ambrosio Castillo in 1936 after the Bolivia-Paraguay war. This is what she told:

Many years ago I was appointed as Commanding Officer to Asuncion, Paraguay. This was a great opportunity for a young officer and for any young person wishing to render vital service for God.

One day, whilst going about the household tasks, there came a knock at the door. When I answered it, I found a man who to my great surprise, without any preliminaries, asked: "What must I do to be saved?" I invited him into our meeting hall at the side of the house, read to him from my Bible and later prayed with him. The man left our house overcome with emotion but with a new experience in his heart.

I told him he must bring his family to the meetings; he replied that it would be impossible, as they did not live in the city but on an island, and the traveling was expensive. I thought it was my duty to go to the island to visit them, so one day I set out. It was indeed a difficult journey and an expensive one. I spoke with the man's wife and children about the salvation that Christ offered, if they would only believe, and they became convinced of their need of conversion.

On later visits it wasn't the Castillo family only (that was their name) but, as the man himself suggested, all the neighbors also were invited to attend the meetings. In Paraguay the nights are beautiful, clear, and bright, and by the light of the moon we sang the [Salvation] Army songs and read together God's Word. In subsequent months many converts came from this little place.

What happened next came as a surprise. One day Señor Castillo said to me, "Captain, did you know that I am a leper?" "Leper!" I repeated, "but surely you know that the authorities are continually asking that all lepers present themselves, to be transferred to the leprosarium? It is your responsibility now as a Christian to do this." "Yes," he replied, "I know that is. what I must do, but there is something more. I have this lovely family, but I am not married."

I had the privilege of conducting the wedding ceremony of this couple. Then one day I said to Señor Castillo, "We have to go to the authorities so that you might fulfill the law." It was a very sad farewell. The family and the comrades had shared some wonderful blessings in that island home.

After this I was transferred to another city and later married. When my husband and I were appointed as the district officers to Paraguay, I thought of the Castillo family. After inquiring I found that our comrade was still in the leprosarium, so we went to visit him. What a surprise awaited us!

We saw a little ranch-type house, built of wood, outside it a noticeboard with the faded letters, *Ejército de Salvación* ["Salvation Army"]. We entered this tiny home and found inside a Salvation Army flag, very old and faded. Here, Señor (now Sergeant) Castillo

maintained his firm witness as a Salvationist. This home was the center of the outpost of which he was in charge, and from him the victims of leprosy heard the Word of God preached.

With him was a son, who also had the disease. There was a little harmonium on which to play Army songs, but the son showed us his hands, saying, "We have a harmonium; but now it is impossible for me to play it because my fingers have fallen off. But I go with my father on his visitation, as he is almost blind because of the disease. I help him read the Bible and the songs, and lead the meeting. Now that I cannot play, the least I can do is sing. I must do something for the honor and glory of God."

This is the last we heard of faithful Ambrosio Castillo.

As for Maria herself, she was declared free of leprosy in 1955/56 and was allowed in 1974 to immigrate to the United States. She is now in her eighty-seventh year and is in moderately good health as a beloved sister at one of our Bruderhofs in the USA, where she lived with her dear husband until his death in December 1985. In 1978 the couple experienced their golden wedding anniversary happily together after many years of separation.

# GLOSSARY OF SPANISH TERMS

*alegría f* joy, gladness
*arco iris m* rainbow
*arroyo m* stream, brook
*asado m* roast
*bombilla f* a small tube with a strainer at one end, used in drinking maté
*bueno -a adj* good
*calabozo m* jail, prison
*camillero -a mf* stretcher bearer, ward attendant
*campesino m* countryman
*campo m* prairie
*chacra f* small farm, smallholding
*compañero -a mf* companion, partner, common-law husband or wife
*enfermero -a mf* nurse
*estanciero m* rancher, cattle raiser
*galleta f* hardtack
*galpón m* shed, barn
*gordo -a adj* plump, fat
*leproso -a mf* leper
*letrado -a adj* learned, wise
*machete m* bush or cane knife
*maté m* an aromatic beverage prepared in Paraguay from the leaves of the Paraguay tea (*Ilex paraguayensis*). It resembles tea and coffee in its stimulant properties.
*pabellón m* pavilion, hospital ward
*pasatiempo m* pastime
*puchero m* stew, pot
*ranchito m* small hut, one-roomed dwelling
*reunión f* meeting, gathering
*sala f* hall, dormitory
*sano -a adj* healthy
*Servicio Tecnico Interamericano de Cooperación Agrícola* (STICA) Inter-American Technical Service of Agricultural Cooperation
*tereré m* maté made with cold water and sucked through a bombilla
*tonto -a adj* stupid, foolish
*viejo -a adj* old
*yuyo m* herb, weed

Doña M.